How to Deal With
POWERFUL
PERSONALITIES

Other books by Tim Kimmel
Raising Kids Who Turn Out Right
Homegrown Heroes: How to Raise Courageous Kids
Little House on the Freeway
Surviving Life in the Fast Lane (a discussion guide for *Little House on the Freeway*)

Videos by Tim Kimmel
"Building Confident Families"
"Building Close Families"
"Building Calm Families"

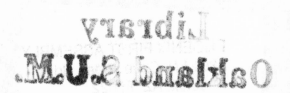

How to Deal With

POWERFUL PERSONALITIES

DR. TIM KIMMEL

PUBLISHING
Colorado Springs, Colorado

HOW TO DEAL WITH POWERFUL PERSONALITIES
Copyright © 1994 by Tim Kimmel
All rights reserved. International copyright secured.

Library of Congress Cataloging-in-Publication Data
    Kimmel, Dr. Tim
    How to Deal with powerful personalities/Tim Kimmel
      p. cm.
    ISBN 1-56179-385-X
    1. Control (Psychology). 2. Autonomy (Psychology). 3. Interpersonal relations.
4. Family—Psychological aspects. 5. Interpersonal relations—Religious aspects—Christianity.
6. Family—Religious life. I. Title.
    BF632.5K55 1993
    144.2'32—dc20

                                      93-6795
                                      CIP

Published by Focus on the Family, Colorado Springs, Colorado 80995

Distributed in U.S.A. and Canada by Word Books, Dallas, Texas.

Unless otherwise noted, Scripture taken from the New American Standard Bible. © 1960, 1962,
1963, 1968, 1971, 1972, 1973, 1975, 1977 by the Lockman Foundation. Used by permission.

Some people's names and certain details of case studies mentioned in this book have been changed
to protect the privacy of the individuals involved.

Permissions
        Chapter Thirteen: "You've Got a Friend," by Carole King.
        Chapter Fourteen: Adapted from the poem "Here's to Kids Who Are Different,"
        by Digby Wolfe. Used by permission.

Editor: Gwen Weising
Designer: Jeff Stoddard
Cover Illustration: Jeff Stoddard

Printed in the United States of America

    95 96 97 98 99/10 9 8 7 6 5 4 3 2 1

This book is dedicated to all the people who, throughout the ages, have been controlled to death.

Tim Kimmel conducts parenting and men's conferences throughout the United States. For more information about his seminars or his availability as a speaker, write or call:

Tim Kimmel
Generation Ministries
P.O. Box 31031
Phoenix, AZ 85046
(602) 948-2545

Acknowledgments

I owe a special thanks to some bigger-than-life people:

Mark Holmlund, for the keys to his kingdom
by the sea. Glenn Rosenberger, for an afternoon that
moved my idea from the theoretical to the practical.
Bill and Ann Epley, for giving me a place to dust and
polish the manuscript.
Gwen Weising, for her compassionate editing.
My sweet wife, Darcy, who never stopped believing
and encouraging me through this process.
Karis, Cody, Shiloh, and Colt, for making going home
at night the highlight of my life.

Table of Contents

Part One

CHAPTER 1

Hostages in the Home

ynthia cringed as her mother hugged her. It was going to be a difficult spring break. Twenty-two years of being her mother's "little girl" had long since worn thin. She couldn't believe how much she could love and despise the same woman—but she did. She loved the woman she longed for her mother to be, and she despised the mother she was.

Now, standing in the entryway of the house where she had grown up, she felt like a stranger. For 22 years she'd lived, breathed, talked, and played out her mother's every wish. During those years, she could not recall a single time when she had felt anything remotely close to freedom. She was shackled—a hostage in her own home—to the smothering control of her mother who refused to let go.

She was still stinging from all the pain she'd had to endure in the last five months. Her emotions were close to the edge. If she didn't take a stand against her mother's control soon, she would plunge into an emotional hole from which she might never extricate herself.

Five months before the fuse had been lit for the explosion, she decided to change her hair to its natural color. Although a towhead at birth, during her teenage years her hair turned darker. The stylist who cut her hair during that time told Cynthia's mother it is quite normal for blonde children to become brunette adults. But her mother couldn't accept what he said. For some unknown reason, she decided "her little girl" looked best as a blonde and that nothing, not even God's genetic programming, was going to interfere with her conviction. That's when she began to have Cynthia's hair frosted. A decade later, she was still having it done.

One year, when she returned to the university after summer break, Cynthia felt it was time for a change. She was tired of color touch-ups, tired of the hassle, and most of all, tired of being a 22-year-old woman who didn't have any say in her own life.

That's what provoked her to have her hair colored to her natural shade of brown. In one sweeping move, she figured she could solve several problems at once. But two weeks later, she went home to attend a cousin's wedding shower. When she pulled into the driveway of her parents' home, her mother came out to meet her and screamed when she got a good look at Cynthia's hair. In fact, Cynthia wasn't even out of the car when she heard the shrill litany begin.

"What happened to my baby? What happened to my little girl? Cynthia, what on earth were you thinking? The sparkle's gone from your eyes. That color makes your complexion look horrible. It just isn't *you*. You were meant to be a blonde!"

On and on it went throughout the weekend. Cynthia resisted when her mother ordered her to make an immediate appointment to change her hair back to blonde. She sat quietly alone at the wedding shower when her mother refused to "attend a social event with a stranger." And she cried as she drove back to the university.

Then there was the fuss her mother made about Cynthia's sorority pictures. Her mom refused to purchase them and forbade Cynthia to buy any for herself. She further infected the wound with a stunt she pulled at her cousin's wedding. Since there was a professional photographer present, Cynthia's mother decided to have a family picture taken for their Christmas card. As Cynthia snuggled in next to her brothers and sisters, her mother called to her to "sit this one out." As Cindy sat down behind the photographer, her mother yelled out, "I don't have time to write a letter to all our friends explaining what happened to my precious little girl." The pleas of Cynthia's siblings had no impact. Her mother simply told them to mind their own business and say cheese.

Cynthia couldn't take it any longer. She desperately wanted her mother's approval. So when she returned to the university after Thanksgiving break, she made an appointment to have her hair turned back to blonde. She then called her mother to say she was weary of the battle and ready to surrender.

But it wasn't over. Cynthia couldn't believe what happened next. Just as her hairdresser began shampooing her hair, he was called to the phone. It was her mother, calling long distance to give him specific instructions about Cynthia's hair.

Now, a few weeks later, standing in the entryway of her house, surrounded by the familiar sights and smells of home, Cynthia stiffened to her mother's embrace. Listening to her go on and on about how her "little girl's eyes sparkle again" made her want to throw up.

Now she understood why her father had left. The reasons were perfectly clear why her mother's second husband was also in the process of moving out. But for Cynthia, it wasn't as simple as walking away. The issues were complicated. Her mother had run her life from day one, and she felt powerless to do anything about it. She was the unwitting victim of "smother love," that kind of love that consumes a spirit and makes someone the completion of another person's expectations. Cynthia was deeply wounded in heart by the person she needed most.

Who Goes There, Friend or Foe?

This book is the result of prolonged staring at a phenomenon that is as much a part of our everyday lives as eating. It is control. The book grew out of a series of encounters—counseling cases, mainly—where control was a factor. One of those was with the teenage boy who felt he couldn't breathe without his father's permission. His athletic, academic, and social schedule had to pass his father's approval or else. And then there was the eight-year-old girl with ulcers. She had become the ointment that soothed the pain of her mother's battered childhood. She was the validation to the world that her mother could do something right. But the explosive nature of her mother's disappointments had made an emotional and physical wreck of her.

The human tendency is to control. The number of people hurt by it is higher than any of us care to count. The more I stared at the problem, the more I began to see how devastating control's effects are on those who are controlled. For too many, control is the drug of the 1990s. Those powerful personalities feel the only way to be under control is by being in control. And usually, that control is exercised at some other person's expense.

There's nothing wrong with power. There's nothing wrong with having a strong personality. In fact, one of the things missing in our culture today is strong, ethical leadership—especially in our homes. We long for a generation of leaders who don't lick their fingers and hold them to the wind when you ask what they believe. The issues that plague us cry out for people who make their decisions from a position of power and strength rather than from the depth of their insecurities.

But what happens when strength steps over the line? When it abuses its privileges and punishes with its power? Although many cultural enemies (crowded schedules, redefined roles, information overload, etc.) undermine relationships, their negative influence can be minimal compared to the overwhelming damage done by high-control individuals wielding authority over others' spirits.

Behind the Olan Mills portraits of so many American families are individuals grinding their teeth from the tension of years and years of being controlled. Everything looks fine to an outsider viewing those families, but to those enduring daily life at the mercy of a controlling, smothering personality, life is lonely and exasperating.

It's not an overstatement to suggest that this problem exists to some extent in all families. The tendency to control is basic to humanity. It's that inner need for one personality to protect itself through the strength it can leverage against another. Control is not healthy for either the controller or the one being controlled. It blunts the controller's capacity to love, but more than that, it also limits the capabilities and the capacity to dream of the one being controlled. We may love to control others, but we hate it when anyone controls us.

We each function in several key circles of support: work, church, school, interest groups, close friends, and, last but most important, the family. High-control bosses, manipulative managers, power-broker pastors, influence-peddling friends, and controlling family members slip through the cracks of our personalities and suck out our potential. They put our individuality in a straitjacket and take it upon themselves to redefine us according to their whims.

This book explores the thin line between love and control—the control that happens when leaders muscle, nurturers panic, lovers selfishly manipulate, and one family member violates the values and *value* of another family member. It's about relationships under siege from within, individuals held hostage by the people they love and count on the most. And it's written to help those who harm as well as those who are hurt—to help them understand how overcontrol murders the human spirit. It offers understanding and hope to both kinds of people.

Scattered throughout the pages of this book are keys showing the oppressor and the oppressed how they can unchain themselves from punishing personalities. They'll learn how to free themselves, their families, and all those with whom they associate to be all God intended them to be.

A Word to the Wise

Before you make a commitment to reading the pages that follow, I need to explain a few things. This isn't going to be a clinical work on the subject of control. There are two reasons for that. First, I don't like to read clinical books (even though I read many of them while preparing to write this one). Second, I enjoy even less having to write them. Life is too short, time is too valuable, and most people are too easily bored to spend a lot of time reading a complicated treatment of any subject. I'll leave all the psycho-verbiage and controlled test cases for the "shrinks" and sociologists to debate at their next convention. I live my life at street level, and I'm writing this book for other people whom I rub shoulders with as I walk through life.

There's another thing I need to tell you. I'm refusing to take on the role of an authority on this subject. Authorities, by their very definition, tend to be too rigid. They work from the position of a mind that's made up—often at the expense of practicality. The subject of controlling personalities is too big and too complicated to be distilled down to a few pat formulas. If I'm anything, I'm a veteran on the subject of control. For more than 20 years I've watched it, experienced it, practiced it, suffered from it, and worked side by side with people who are plagued by it. If I have any expertise, it's because I've been looking at control a little closer than the average guy out there, and I've learned a few things in the process. Those things are here in this book, and they can help you if you'll let them.

One last thing you need to know about me is that I'm a family man. I'm one of those guys who'd rather take his kids to play in the plastic balls at McDonald's than stay at home and wax his hood ornament. I get a bigger kick out of making s'mores in the living room fireplace with the family than I do from having power lunches with big clients. I've been married to the same woman for more than two decades, and I'd rather spend an evening with her accomplishing absolutely nothing than sitting around a boardroom figuring out how to corner the market.

Don't get me wrong. I know who butters my bread. I realize corporate America isn't some warm, fuzzy encounter group. I have my ladders to climb, my goals to pursue, and my share of challengers' rear ends to kick. But a friend of mine said that "the meek shall inherit the earth," and I believe Him.

There's nothing weak about meek people. It's just that their strength lies in dimensions of life that are hard to come by and easy to lose. It's wrapped in the breadth of their character, the depth of their convictions, and the height of their ideals. It takes years to develop and can't be quantified on your résumé. These strengths are what I most respect in others and most long for in my own life. The people who have qualities of strength are the true movers and shakers of life. They have a way of empowering relationships and bringing out the best in the people they love.

So this book comes from the context of my marriage, my four children, the friendships that surround me, the professional circles in which I move, and the homework I've done in preparation for writing. I believe this book has the potential to set spirits free. It will do so two ways:

first, by helping individuals see themselves either as controlling or controlled persons, and second, by offering solutions to their oppressing or oppressed relationships.

Join me on a pilgrimage. It's a journey that will get easier the further we go as, one by one, we unlock the shackles of control that have imprisoned your heart. Come. Follow me down the trail to relationships based on grace rather than control.

CHAPTER 2

When Push Comes to Shove

Harley winced and checked his watch while shifting his weight in the chair. He wished the esteemed senator from Ohio would just shut up so the chairman could drop his gavel and adjourn the subcommittee for the weekend. His battle with the "Big C" was now four years old, and he finally understood why someone had invented the expression "the cure is worse than the disease." Radiation treatments and chemotherapy had fried his insides.

However, as bad as the cancer was, it was a secondary distraction. He had accepted the fact that dying was part of living, and if his number was about to be called, then so be it. What preoccupied his waking hours was avoiding the team of investigative reporters that had been shadowing him for the past six weeks.

Harley was a senior staff member of this Senate subcommittee. He'd been working in Washington, D.C., for more than ten years and had climbed the bureaucratic ladder to an enviable position. But a staff member was not one of the big shots who made the decisions. Why couldn't the reporters recognize that and pick on someone their own size?

Their pen became mightier than his sword when they turned the focus of their "watchdog" column on this Senate subcommittee. They really weren't after Harley; they'd made that clear from the outset. But unless he released the "dirt" they needed to put a certain senator from the Northwest out of commission, Harley was going to be the "sacrificial lamb." (That was *their* terminology.) The last four columns these reporters had sent to their syndicators had raised questions about Harley's role in the committee. Nothing immoral had been revealed. For that matter, they had reported nothing that was at all unusual for Capitol Hill. But the doubts they raised about him had their desired effect. The phone in his office had been ringing constantly for almost two weeks. Just one more negative column with his name in it and Harley would have no choice but to resign his hard-earned government position.

As for the senator from the Northwest, Harley wasn't going to give the reporters what they wanted for two reasons. First, there *wasn't* any dirt to offer—at least not the kind they were looking for. They were certain the senator was crooked, on the take, and using his position to line the pockets of his cronies back home. It wasn't true, at least not so far as Harley could see.

The senator did have one plaguing problem, but it wasn't corruption. It was whiskey. He was a "pluperfect," face-in-porcelain, sick-as-a-brick drunk. But that was no big secret. Anyone who was around him for very long could figure that out. He was unreliable at times, and the drinking obviously affected his personal judgment. He managed to survive because, for the most part, he followed the advice of his staff. Even if he did act presumptuously sometimes, his actions did little harm, because he had only one vote at the committee level.

The second reason Harley wouldn't cooperate in bringing down this senator was loyalty. The senator was his friend. They'd known each other long before either had ever thought of heading for Washington. Although backstabbing was as much a part of the games being played within the Washington Beltway as Redskins football, Harley wasn't going to participate. Friendship still meant something to him. He wasn't going to give the political columnists the gossip they wanted to hang his friend out to dry. But he had to pay a price for his loyalty.

The words from one of the columnists were echoing in Harley's head: "If you don't give me what I want, you're going down." He probably

10

shouldn't have responded with an expletive, but it came out before he thought about it. He just wished he could get a reprieve from having to fight for his job all the time so that he could give his full attention to fighting for his life.

Headlines and Bullies

I remember the day I picked up *The Arizona Republic* and read the headlines announcing Harley's resignation. The article was full of bullying, sensational quotations, and slanted information. The investigative reporter was scalp hunting, and Harley's was better than none. He knew Harley was just a pawn in a big game, but the greater goal of nailing the senator seemed to justify his chewing up an innocent bystander.

What happened to Harley has happened over and over again throughout history. The world has suffered from bullies ever since Cain and Abel were born. History is, in large part, the story of control brokers intimidating the weak and defenseless. The closer I look at the subject of control, the more I realize we've all got a little touch of this disease. Deep within our complex makeup is the urge to protect ourselves. And one of the most well-worn weapons we reach for is control. It's used in key relationships at the office, in the dugout at the Tuesday night softball games, in car pools, and as we sit around the dinner table. It can be subtle and annoying or blatant and devastating. Harley found his power taken from him by someone who had no qualms about abusing influence. What he experienced in a major way is what many rank-and-file people experience in varying degrees every day.

You can see why I was compelled to learn more about this subject. Surrounded by it every day as I counseled, I wanted to know the cause as well as the antidote to the damage that overcontrol has on people. So I set out on a fact-finding mission.

In my research, I found that although the psychiatric community is aware of the problem, very little has been written to define, develop, and offer help to the culprits or victims of overcontrol.

Next I turned to the theological libraries. It seemed to me that something as universal as control abuse would have enjoyed an exhaustive discussion in religious literature. But the books were unusually quiet on the subject. That made sense after I thought about it a while. One of the flaws of the Christian movement is its propensity to use its belief system to manipulate those outside and muscle those within. I seldom have to go very far with a church before I find someone bending one of the sheep's legs behind its back and making it scream "uncle." Sometimes the man handling the lamb is wearing a clerical collar. But it cuts both ways, and sometimes the one crying "uncle" is not a sheep but a shepherd. The list of pastors who have been the main course at the deacons' feeding frenzy is endless. (We'll talk more about this in a chapter on evangelical power brokers.)

If a church were to try to understand, from the Bible, God's perspective on the subject of control, it might eliminate one of its best instruments to keep the "cause" and its followers on the straight and narrow. It's far easier to coerce people into obedience than to love them into it. It's probably the same reason I likewise found very little written on the problem of overcontrol from the family perspective.

I wanted to know what control is and what the Bible has to say about it. I wanted to know why and how we control. Ultimately, this knowledge would enable me to draw some conclusions about those who control and those who are forced to look down the barrel of the controller's gun.

I think you'll find what I discovered in the Bible interesting. The discovery gave me a wide-eyed look into the heart of God. And with that look came urgent applications for my own life. My wife, my children, and my friends were the immediate beneficiaries.

Stepping Back to Take It All In

Try on the following statement to see how it fits: *Most people abuse power by negatively controlling people around them.*

Those who agree with this statement tend to be aware enough of their urge to control that they make a regular effort to keep it in check. Those who disagree tend to be some of its greatest abusers.

We don't like it, but controlling tendencies are part of the fundamental makeup of the human heart. Very early in life, we learn ways to avoid or relieve the discomforts of daily living by flexing the muscles of our personalities for personal gain. When our first temper tantrum gets results, we learn that we can get people who are bigger than us to submit to our agenda. When we see how quickly favors follow compliments wrapped in charm, we learn the power of affection and praise in getting our own way. And when our background is crowded with people who have taken control to an art form, it's hard to avoid adding it to our own emotional repertoire.

Asking the Right Questions

When I'm wrestling with some of the great dilemmas of life, I like to start my search for answers in the one Book that has stood the test of time—the Bible. My walk through God's Word established the premise for this book. But before I could find what I was looking for, I needed a clear definition of control. After all, some forms of control are obviously acceptable and necessary. Emergencies, certain vocational and positional responsibilities, and moral dilemmas sometimes call for a take-charge attitude. Those are legitimate uses of control. They aren't selfishly motivated. In those cases, we're not taking the position of control to act in our own best interests.

For our discussion, therefore, let me define control this way:

Control is when you leverage the strength of your position or personality against the weakness of someone else's in order to get that person to meet your selfish agenda.

With pen and pad in hand, I took my definition of control to the Bible and tried it out on the people and events found there. Mainly I wanted to see how often selfish control turned out well and how often it backfired. Starting in Genesis, I listed various interactions of people who fit the definition of control and checked whether the end result was good or bad. For example:

- The snake tried to control Eve . . . bad—sin entered the world.
- Eve tried to control Adam . . . bad—they both lost their innocence.

13

- Adam tried to control God . . . bad—he lost paradise.
- Cain tried to control Abel . . . bad—it resulted in the first murder.
- Abraham tried to control Sarah (regarding Pharaoh) . . . bad—he made liars out of everyone.
- Sarah tried to control Hagar . . . bad—the Mideast conflict was born.
- Rebekah tried to control Jacob . . . bad—she turned him into a professional liar.
- Jacob tried to control Esau . . . bad—it resulted in a permanent family feud.

On and on the pattern went. Every time someone in the Bible tried to use the strength of his personality against the weakness of someone else, it turned out badly. I couldn't find a single example of a person controlling another and arriving at good results. If space permitted, I could go on and on listing some of the most famous and infamous people in the Bible who caused major problems when they turned to cunning or coercion to get what they wanted.

From what I saw, I believe it's safe to assume *God never intended one person to control another.* He didn't wire us to respond well to it, either. In each of our hearts is an innate aversion to a person or persons from the outside *compelling* us to do things that primarily benefit them. Our spirits automatically resist or, if they have no choice, become overwhelmed by a sense of bondage within the relationship. Either way, controlling personalities contribute to the human nightmare and fall far short of God's intention.

Discovering this provoked another set of questions in me. "What about Jesus? What did He do?" After all, He was God in the flesh. It seems fair to assume that if anyone had the authority, power, and right to control, it was Jesus. Therefore, if anyone could show us the boundaries on this issue, it would be Him. So, using the same definition and methodology, I went to the Gospels to study the life of Christ. I wanted to list all the times He leveraged the strength of His personality against the weakness of another's in order to get a personal agenda met.

You probably already know what I discovered. I couldn't find a single such incident. Not one! Jesus never controlled anyone. He never took advantage of His position. And, as a result, He modeled the exact relationship that God the Father maintains with us. He lets us know where the boundaries are and what He desires, but the action we take is our choice. If Jesus didn't control anyone, even though He had the right, we *shouldn't* control people either. When we do, it doesn't turn out well. It's an unwarranted position we've taken within a relationship at the expense of the other person.

We aren't supposed to control our spouses. We aren't supposed to control our children. The Bible says we're to keep them *under* control, and as we'll see in a later chapter, there's a big difference between controlling children and keeping them under control.

The foundational principle that leaped at me from the Scriptures is that control, as we've defined it here, is destructive and evil. It fuels rage within others. It handicaps and even paralyzes their abilities and potentials. And it is counter to the way God meant us to be.

That's why, of all the places from which we want to exorcise this destructive force, the most important is the home. Home determines too many outcomes in life. It is the most effective environment for good or evil in the world. Essayist Lance Morrow summed it up this way:

> The womb is the first home. Thereafter, home is the soil you come from and recognize, what you knew before being uprooted; creatures carry an imprint of home, a stamp—the infinitely subtle distinctiveness of temperature and smell and weather and noises and people, the intonations of the familiar. Each home is an unrepeatable configuration; it has personality, its own emanation, its spirit of place. . . . Home is one of nature's primal forms, and if it does not take shape properly around the child, then his mind will be at least a little homeless all its life.[1]

In the two decades your children will live under the shade of your love, what is the most important quality you want them to learn from you? There are many noble character traits, but if they aren't seasoned with grace, those qualities will not imprint your children's souls the way you would like. Selfish control is the antithesis of grace. It will not only undermine the good qualities you are trying to build into your children, but it will also blunt

God's efforts in their hearts.

When we marry, we exchange vows to love and to cherish until some day one lays the other into the arms of God. Selfish control can make people within a marriage die emotionally in advance of their natural death. Their spirits give up hope, and the rest of the marriage experience is merely enduring until the end. Someone has said that you're either doubled or halved the day you get married. If you marry into a high-control relationship, you will find yourself at less than half.

Whether in the home front or the marketplace, the boardroom or the bedroom, the best relationship is one in which personalities are committed to setting hearts free. Is your heart a haven for bonding or bondage? Are the relationships that mean the most to you building a sense of deeply rooted confidence, or are people within your circle of influence suffering from a "sense of homelessness"—that feeling of confusion when the love exchanged has too many conditions attached?

The good news is that, regardless of the answers to those questions, you can positively affect the future. You *can* have grace-based relationships, free from the encumbrances of control. But this requires a willingness to be vulnerable, and vulnerability is the archenemy of both those who control and those who are controlled.

The following is a list of questions meant to help you evaluate your potential for control. Answer them as honestly as you can, and after you do, have someone close to you answer them on your behalf. See how well his viewpoint and yours match. You are about to learn something important about yourself.

1. When things seem to be getting out of control, do you tend to "take charge" because you trust your ability to make things turn out right more than you do the ability of those close to you?

Yes_____   No_____

2. When you don't get your way, do feelings rise up within you—anger, fear, or maybe shame?

Yes_____   No_____

3. Do you think, *It's all up to me. If I don't do it, it won't get done?*
Yes_____   No_____

4. Does the thought *They never seem to do it right* sometimes cross your mind when dealing with your associates, spouse, or children?
Yes_____   No_____

5. Do the people close to you tend to defer to you for the last word on their plans or dreams?
Yes_____   No_____

6. Do the people you care about the most feel their thoughts, suggestions, or desires can gain an objective hearing from you?
Yes_____   No_____

7. If people's opinions of you are important, do you use any personality strengths to manipulate their opinions without their knowing it?
Yes_____   No_____

8. Do you find it easy to accept being out-voted when plans are being formulated within your circle of relationships?
Yes_____   No_____

9. When you pray, do you suggest solutions to your dilemmas to God?
Yes_____   No_____

10. When you're around powerful people, do you feel a strong urge to try to "beat them at their own game"?
Yes_____   No_____

How did your responses to these questions concur with your child's or your spouse's evaluation of you? The strong urge to control may be so much a part of your life that you don't even notice it. But others do, and they are strongly affected by it.

What about those who find themselves on the receiving end? The next set of questions will help you determine if your tendencies fall on the side of being controlled by others:

1. Do you feel that your opinions carry much weight with the people close to you?
Yes_____   No_____

2. When things seem out of control, do you prefer someone else to solve the problem?
Yes_____   No_____

3. Are you free to make most of the major decisions that confront you each day without gaining the approval of your spouse, parent, or closest friend?
Yes_____   No_____

4. When you spend a lot of time around people you love the most (spouse, parent, friends), do they make you feel free and unconfined inside?
Yes_____   No_____

5. Do you feel as though it's difficult to consistently please the person or people closest to you?
Yes_____   No_____

6. Do you live by the motto "Peace at any price"?
Yes_____   No_____

7. Is your future outlook exciting rather than gloomy?
Yes_____   No_____

8. Do you have a difficult time responding lovingly to the person or people you care for the most?
Yes_____   No_____

9. Do you feel empowered (better about yourself and your abilities) by the people closest to you?
Yes_____   No_____

10. Do you feel too threatened to voice your frustration when the people close to you leverage the strength of their personalities against you?
Yes_____   No_____

Nobody wants to be controlled. It puts nothing into us and takes a lot out. God's design is for us to develop relationships that empower us and others—relationships that draw out the best in everyone involved. God wants us to be free, especially within the confines of our families. And whether we're the controllers or the controlled, He can enable us to enjoy the same freedom that the apostle Paul experienced when God told him, *"My grace is sufficient for you, for power is perfected in weakness"* (2 Corinthians 12:9).

If you want to learn the weaknesses that fuel controlling spirits, turn the page. God wants to perfect His power through our weaknesses.

CHAPTER 3

The High Cost of Control

I wish I could wire this book so that as soon as you start reading this paragraph, a certain song would whistle from the pages. And if you could hear that tune, I'm fairly confident I could predict the images that would drift across the front wall of your mind:

Andy Taylor and his son, Opie, walking home from the fishing hole.

Otis staggering into the sheriff's office and locking himself in jail long enough to sleep off his hangover.

Gomer worrying about spider bites.

Aunt Bea offering her friend Clara a second piece of homemade apple pie.

The Andy Griffith Show is so enduring because it's so endearing. It's like a good-fitting pair of hiking boots with which we refuse to part. It conjures up a townful of people and a tone of life for which most of us long, a place of quiet and stability.

But believe it or not, the program was also a great metaphor for control. We saw ourselves in the characters of that tender show. There was a little of us in them. They personified our greatest strengths and our sorriest weaknesses, and they helped us get a chuckle out of both. Of the characters who made up that timeless sitcom, none breathed more life into the series than Deputy Bernard (Barney) P. Fife.

Barney and the Lone Bullet

High-control personalities are incidents waiting to happen and accidents needing to be minimized. The people we love provide the relationships we depend on for joy and meaning. But high-control personalities tread a thin line between the rights we grant them and the liberties they usurp. And Barney Fife is their patron saint.

He's lovable and laughable—a tightly wound spring with military creases and a badge. From the beginning of the series until the end, Barney longed for the authority to control the lives of the people around him. Had Sheriff Taylor allowed him to, he would have incarcerated without mercy, interrogated without sensitivity, and sentenced without grace. Andy recognized Barney's well-intentioned motives but consistently curtailed his poorly timed outbursts.

One of the best running gags in television history had to do with the bullet Barney kept in his shirt pocket. That's the closest Andy allowed Barney to get to deadly force. Andy insisted that Barney keep an empty gun in his holster and a single bullet in his shirt pocket. In absolute emergencies, the gun and bullet could be matched up; otherwise, they were to be kept apart. Andy knew Barney was too quick to draw his gun and too anxious to shove its barrel under somebody's nose. He also knew Barney was his own worst enemy. A loaded gun was almost always an assurance that somewhere along the line, Deputy Fife would shoot himself in the foot.

As we deal with the high-control personalities around us, we find that most of the time their guns are loaded. And too often, we find ourselves looking down the barrels of those guns.

It takes only one unchecked Barney Fife at the office to zap the joy out of our workday. A manager that's high on authority and low on poise (a keen sense of the appropriate) can demotivate us enough to send us looking through the help-wanted ads regularly. A single cocksure boss can do more to stifle a company's potential and its employees' ideas than any downward turn in the economy. High-control authorities in the workplace do more harm to a company's bottom line than the stockholders could ever imagine. The marketplace, like history, has been the study of misaligned influence and mismanaged authority.

I believe that the companies standing the best chance of survival in the fickle economies of the twenty-first century will be those that promote humble managers and servant leaders—men and women who use their position and authority to empower and motivate others rather than themselves.

But work may not be the only place where we encounter a Barney Fife. We may walk out the door of our workplace at five o'clock each evening and forget about the high-control personality there. But what about the Barneys with whom we live? How do we cope with those who are reading the paper in the family room or struggling with an algebra problem at the dining room table? Or perhaps, though we hate to face it, we need to discipline *ourselves* to keep our bullets in our pockets. The sad truth is that home is where the greatest abuses in power and influence are committed against our most intimate relationships.

The powerful personalities who whittle away at the foundation of our families cannot be ignored. Those controlling people have an uncanny ability to format our dreams and harass our hopes.

It happened at Sissy's house. Hers was no *Mayberry, RFD* scenario; it was more like *Nightmare on Elm Street*.

The Games People Play

When I started working with Sissy, her life had been distilled down to a handful of predictable patterns. Her actions when she came home from school were a case in point. She'd mouth a quiet hello to her mother as she passed through the kitchen on her way to her bedroom. Plopping her books on the bed and her purse on the dresser, Sissy would immediately pull off her school clothes. If they weren't dirty, she'd carefully hang them in the closet, being meticulous to return them to the hangers and places on the rod from which she'd taken them that morning. Messing up the color-coordinated closet system her mother was so proud of was too costly. Usually she'd slip into a T-shirt and some shorts and give herself a quick look in the mirror. She had a hard time respecting what was looking back at her.

Her next moves were equally habitual. Her actions had nothing to do with any highly developed set of internal disciplines. They were merely coping mechanisms. Sissy would sit down at her desk, slide her books across her bed, organize them, and then proceed to tear into her homework—whether she had any or not. She'd do her current assignments, redo worksheets from the past, or simply feign that she was busy. And just in case, she'd open her Bible to the Psalms (any psalm would do) and set it on the bed beside her.

All this activity was devised to guarantee privacy from her mother. She learned a long time ago that the two things that could keep her mother out of her room were homework and Bible reading. If Mom did stick her head in the door, she'd see Sissy doing what was expected of her. She'd smile and leave her alone. If Sissy wasn't busy, her mother would open her mouth and suck the oxygen out of the room.

Sissy knew her actions were a charade. But she thought she could make it if she could keep up the pretense until graduation, just two years away. Then she could move in with her sister. Regardless of what her parents said at that point, there would be little they could do to stop her.

It had been three years since her sister ran away, and two and a half since her sister's baby was born. Sissy knew her sister had more spunk than she did. She, at least, had stood up to their parents in ways Sissy could not. But in the end, she felt her sister had lost much more than she had gained. In fact, everyone had lost—her sister, her parents, and Sissy. High control was indeed a high-ticket item.

Sissy blamed her parents for most of what happened. They had driven her sister out of their hearts with their incessant lectures, accusations, and anger. And to frustrate an already frustrating situation, their mother had tried to jam Jesus down both of their throats. Sissy had found herself attracted to the message of the gospel enough to benefit in spite of being force-fed spiritually.

Even though Sissy had not rebelled outwardly, a part of her wanted to strike out against God, if for no other reason than to fire back at her mother. Somehow, however, she was thinking logically enough to reason that by rebelling, she would only hurt herself. It's too bad her sister had not been as logical.

Sissy's father was no stranger to being abusively controlling, either, but he was far more subtle about it than his wife. He matched her aggressive control with equal doses of passive/aggressive control. That's probably why he kept his wife emotionally locked out of his life.

Sissy's dad would come home by six if he didn't stop off for a drink on the way home. If he did, war was inevitable. But if he didn't, war was still a possibility. The conflict would begin when her mother would slip into one of her sanctimonious diatribes about her husband's obvious shortcomings. That would light the fuse. He'd get up from the table without saying a word and go out to the garage to have a shot from the bottle he kept under the front seat of his car. The words Sissy's mother yelled though the garage door fell on deaf ears.

Her mother couldn't see anything wrong with her sermons. She couldn't see that there was never any grace in her words. She seemed to think God was a rope you put around people to keep them in line. Her incessant carping about her husband's spiritual flaws only made them worse, and his passive/aggressive responses (we'll talk about this in a later chapter) seemed only to validate her point—at least in her eyes.

It hadn't always been this bad. Sissy's parents started out like most couples, with common goals and a lot of anticipation. But the high-control tendencies of one partner succeeded in redefining the other until eventually there was little in their relationship that resembled what they'd had when they first fell in love.

Sissy's mother's commitment to minding her entire family's business had turned Sissy into a passive controller. She played a series of head games to counter her mother's control without her mother ever realizing it. She never wanted it this way, but somewhere between her first tooth and getting her braces off, her home had turned into a prison, and she dared not face off with the wardens. What a shame! When they were nice to each other, she could actually see their potential as a family.

I have known Sissy and her family for a long time. I've been able to track the devastating effect that high control has on close relationships. Her parents' pride closed them off to any help. They divorced a few years after Sissy graduated from high school.

Sissy ultimately married, and after a few tough years, she made some great adjustments that seem to be paying off in her roles as wife and mother, as well as in her career. She fared better than her sister, who has failed to corner any long-lasting happiness.

What happened to this family is the result of individuals not solving little problems—flaws—that eventually turned into patterns of control. And this family is much like many others.

Head Games and Heart Songs

People control others because they embrace a handful of false notions. They have a flawed view of love, themselves, others, and God. While they are motivated by good intentions, their marred belief system causes them to do anything *but* good for those around them. They feel others will simply mess everything up unless they take charge of choices for those people. So they pry, meddle, coerce, intimidate, isolate, or use whatever other method works in order to bring about the intended results.

Here are some of the suppositions that motivate this type of thinking:
1. *"I am responsible for the outcome of the lives around me."*[1]
There is no question that what we do will affect the lives of people around us. We wield incredible influence in our children's value systems, belief systems, and character. Our nurturing instincts may cause us to push people toward doing what *we* think is best for them. But our partners and children have minds, gifts, and dreams of their own. We may feel a responsibility for them, but they alone are responsible for their choices. They will bear the consequences of those choices. If we take that personal privilege from them, we circumvent God's design and throw into motion a host of unfortunate consequences. Instead of compounding their potential, we diminish it. Instead of freeing their spirits, we shackle them. Instead of motivating them toward independence, we handcuff them to our whims.

2. *"The only way to get something done right is to do it myself."* [2]
I'd hate to have some divine calculator show me how many times I've said this, not only in my role as a spouse and parent, but also in the workplace. In some situations, there's no doubt that our knowledge and skills are superior to those of other members of our family or office staff. And in certain situations, we are the ones who should do a job to get it done right. But what if our superior skill and knowledge are being leveraged in an area where our loved ones need to develop their own skills or knowledge? There could be something more important going on than just getting the job done right. Sometimes others' half-successful attempts enhance their confidence much more than our sophisticated "best shots" at getting the job done well. If we can step far enough back from this discussion, we'll see that there are lots of these kinds of situations in life—every day.

When do we back off and let those we love learn by experience (or failure)? In the next chapters, I'll provide lists of ways that we interfere in our loved ones' lives, simply because we feel more competent at making those choices for them. But we're actually making choices God intended them to make for themselves.

3. *"If I don't help someone make the right decision, do the right thing, or go to the right places, who will?"* [3]
As long as we make choices and set personal agendas for those around us, we keep them dependent on us. Subconsciously, this is often just what we want. When we seize control of the personal dimensions of loved ones' lives, we cause them to view themselves and their capabilities improperly. Inside they're thinking, *I have no control over my choices. Mom (Dad, my spouse, my friend, my boss) does. She's responsible for my actions, not me. She's driving me to these choices, and they have cost me these consequences.*

It's not in the best interests of a family or work staff to build relationships that *keep* people emotionally, volitionally, or spiritually crippled. Instead, we must want to build the individual spirit within those we love in such a way that they find themselves dependent on God and responsible to themselves for the choices they make.

Independence does that! It says, "I am responsible for my actions, and I am responsible for the effect my actions have on others."

No matter how we slice it, when we assume control in areas of people's lives where God has not privileged us, it inevitably backfires. When we tally the negative effects of controlling some other person's life, it's easy to see why it isn't worth it. Let me list a few reasons:

• Regardless of how wise or well-meaning our control over another person may be, that person has an innate need to be in control of himself. Therefore, he will resist even the most loving suggestions.

• The person we try to control will find it difficult to trust us. Therefore, he will also be reluctant to confide in us.

• We could end up resenting the people we're controlling, because they have become so dependent on us that they're now a burden.

• Ultimately, we will see control affect our ability to enjoy genuine intimacy within our closest relationships. For married couples, high control can destroy their ability to respond in healthy and happy ways in their sexual lives.

• High control destroys the free exchange of confidence and loyalty between parents and children.

• Controlling others' lives can exact a high price physically. The stress of controlling others can make *us* sick.

Obviously, control doesn't pay—it costs. To remove it from our relational repertoire, we need to understand why and how we do it. Then we'll be able to change. The next few chapters will show us *how* we control and how we are controlled. That will be followed by a discussion of the root motivations for abusive control. Once those two major questions have been answered, we can learn how to set free the vital relationships in our lives.

First Things First

I've heard that there are 50 ways to leave your lover, but there are only three general ways to control someone. They are:

aggressive control,

passive control,

passive/aggressive control.

Let's look at how these play out in the relationships that matter most to us. And in the process, we'll learn how to put our bullets in our pockets for good.

Part Two

CHAPTER 4

The Aggressive Controller

When I bring up the subject of high-control personalities with my friends, they invariably assume I'm referring to the type of controllers we're about to discuss in this chapter. They assume that high control equals aggressive control.

Aggressive controllers use volume, size, muscle, or authority to get what they want at other people's expense. Because aggressive controllers' methods are so obvious, they are often confronted by the people close to them for the selfish, damaging, and often obnoxious methods they use. There is no good defense for an aggressive relational style. It's arrogant and wrong.

Most people merely tolerate aggressive controllers. Usually it's the only coping mechanism they feel they have. But tolerating isn't a solution; it's a Band-Aid.

Toleration doesn't diminish the negative impact the aggressive controller's patterns have on those who endure them. Some of the hardest emotional scar tissue to heal is that made by the deep wounds of an aggressive controller.

Let's look at the five predominant forms of aggressive control.

The Manager: Her Loved Ones Feel Like Students

Sometimes called the "mother," this aggressive pattern of control is the most common among women. This happens partly because of the role women play in so many homes. Regardless of all the ways women are being defined in the late twentieth century, when it comes to what goes on inside a home, women still have far more input—control—than men. They normally make more of the decisions regarding the children—their scheduling, diet, clothing, social calendar, and friendships. They also make more of the decisions regarding the contents of the home. This certainly doesn't stop a lot of husbands from playing a manager's role, to a fault, in family members' lives. It's just that for women, because of their multiple responsibilities in the home, it's easy for them to fall into overmanaging.

Take Megan, for instance. When she and Mark first came to me to air their differences, I thought they should be in *Who's Who in Ideal Marriages.* Megan was a competent, disciplined, and hardworking woman. She brought understanding and intelligence to the day-to-day decisions necessary to overseeing her household. Her husband would have been the first to agree that she was highly qualified to run her household. It never bothered Mark that his wife could whip him in mental gymnastics. That's one of the reasons he was attracted to her in the first place. Besides, he knew his position on the playing field of their family, and he played it well. On top of that, where he was strong, he was very strong and lacked no confidence.

But Mark finally wearied of Megan's overbearing control in his daily choices. Like most men, when he stopped by the grocery store to pick up something for Megan, he usually saw other things he would throw into the cart as well. But when he got home, he consistently had to defend his purchases.

"Why did you get that?"

"We don't need that."

"What's so difficult about going to the store, getting what you're supposed to, and leaving?"

He couldn't even go to K-Mart without having her second-guess his choices. He didn't feel free to buy any item, even if it was on sale, for fear it wouldn't pass muster with Megan. This developed into so much of a problem that Mark began giving explanations before he pulled his purchases out of the bag.

"Megan, I'm fairly certain that what I bought is not going to meet with your approval. It seldom does. Nor do I think the reasons I give for buying these things will carry much weight in your mind. They seldom do. But I'm your husband, Honey, not your student, and I want to be free to exercise some choices in this area. I love you too much to let you manage me to death."

One of the more humorous ways Megan managed Mark was in the way he took a shower. Mark, like millions of other Americans, took his shower every morning before work. When he got in the shower, he liked to scrub with a fairly large bar of soap. When the bar got so small that he couldn't lather up as easily as he'd like, Mark's habit was to open the shower door, dig around under the sink, and get a new one. He'd then throw the small piece in the wastebasket.

Megan couldn't stand it. If she was in the bathroom, he knew she'd have something to say to him. "There's still plenty of soap left in this bar. You shouldn't open a new one until this one is completely gone."

Speaking of suds, Mark would light her fuse if he dared to open a new bottle of shampoo before the last drop was out of the old one. On several occasions, he opened the shower door to throw away the old bottle and caught Megan's patronizing lecture. She'd bang out a few drops in her hand while insisting, "There's still plenty in there!"

Furthermore, woe be to Mark if he failed to get the last bit of toothpaste out of the tube. Megan managed even this daily chore. To counter this, Mark took some drastic measures to show just how exasperated he'd become. He set a pair of pliers and tin snips on the shelf above the shower. When she inquired about the tools, he stripped naked, jumped in the shower, clamped the teeth of the pliers onto the tiny sliver of soap, and proceeded to wash under his arms.

"Very funny, Mark!" she said. "And what about these tin snips?"

Mark suddenly got the urge to shampoo his hair. "Darn, Megan," he said, "there's only a few drops left in the bottom. No problem!" He then cut the top off the plastic bottle to get the remainder of the shampoo.

Megan smiled and said, "And what about this little hammer over by the sink?" She held up a small hammer from their son's toy set.

Mark walked to the sink, pounded on the shriveled remains of a toothpaste tube, and got a microscopic amount on his brush. Standing there, stark naked, brushing his teeth with one hand and holding a hammer in the other, Mark finally got to Megan. She broke into a full belly laugh. He'd made his point. They came to me for help with their problem a few days later.

Let's give Megan some credit. She was trying to be a good steward of her family's resources. But her constant control of Mark's choices was destroying his confidence in his ability to do even the most mundane things—like taking a shower!

Megan was turning Mark into a programmed robot. In all her well-intended concerns, she had removed the individuality from his heart. She had controlled and numbed his passions for life. She was also risking a great deal in their sexual relationship. As Barbara DeAngelis says, "Behaving like a mommy is the quickest way to kill passion in your marriage. After all, what man wants to sleep with his mother?"[1]

The kids got managed nearly to death, too. If their choice of clothes didn't meet with Megan's approval, they heard about it. Sometimes she made them change. But even when she didn't, they'd go off to school or to a friend's house feeling insecure about their appearance because of the lecture they'd received. And should they ever try to change something in their rooms without clearing it with her, they knew it wouldn't survive her first gaze. As teenagers, they got to the place where they didn't want to go Christmas shopping with her because she filled them with self-doubt by second-guessing all their choices. Her overmanagement took away all their joy in giving a gift.

Managers do that to people. They're obsessed with treating people close to them like students. This gets extremely complicated if the spouse or child is a substance abuser. Managers clean up, cover up, make up, scold, punish, and then, when all is said and done, accept the abuser back. Many times managers feel frustrated and angry because they "are powerless to change him—and therein lies the trap: It is not up to you to change him—(or clean up for him, for that matter)."[2]

The manager-controller communicates a lack of trust in others when she insists on managing their affairs. She makes others feel as though they're always having to prove themselves. This can result in people's becoming what they're suspected of being—people who can't be trusted.

Managers don't operate under the assumption that they know what's better for another person; they operate under the delusion that they know what's best. According to the manager-controller, there are many excellent ways to achieve the best, but of course, most of those ways are their ways.

We are called to manage our homes and families. The problem comes when we assume so much management of others' lives that we block their ability to learn and grow and so diminish their dignity. The manager who controls to a fault blocks God's ability to work in others' lives and circumvents the excellent lessons they need to learn from the "University of Consequences."

The Monarch: His Loved Ones Are Subjects

There's a God-ordained hierarchy within the home. It's been put there to bring security, stability, and staying power to the relationships that make up the family. God has given parents authority and responsibility over the children. Parents are to protect their children as they move through childhood and to prepare them for adulthood. Their position as parents is to be respected.[3] And although there isn't a hierarchy within marriage, there are unique responsibilities for each partner.[4]

But God made an interesting statement about leadership. Basically, the more responsible your position, the greater a servant you're supposed to be. Let's look at a few verses to get this principle straight from the lips of Jesus:

> *You know that the rulers of the Gentiles lord it over them, and their great men exercise authority over them. It is not so among you, but whoever wishes to become great among you shall be your servant, and whoever wishes to be first among you shall be your slave; just as the Son of Man did not come to be*

*served, but to serve, and to give His life a ransom for
many.*

                                        Matthew 20:25b-28

Along the same lines He said:

*And do not be called leaders; for One is your Leader,
that is, Christ. But the greatest among you shall be
your servant. And whoever exalts himself shall be
humbled; and whoever humbles himself shall be
exalted.*

                                        Matthew 23:10-12

Some homes have individuals whose method of controlling others
resembles that of royalty dealing with their subjects. These individuals
establish a kind of monarchy. It isn't just parents who can do this. Spouses
can do it to each other, and kids can do it to their parents. Monarch-
controllers assume a certain level of privilege that may or may not be
rightfully theirs. Then they leverage it against the wills of those around
them.

Monarch-controller fathers of the 1950s used to sit at the dinner table,
pound their chests, and exclaim, "I'm the king of this house!" They had
mistaken their place at the head of the table for something it was not.
Position was never theirs to use as a way of getting others to meet their
selfish agenda. The 1960s dethroned most of the remaining kings of the
baby boomers. But their offspring are still trying the same stunt on their
children.

We use the monarch style of control when we communicate to our
children that they hold an inferior position to ours. They feel it when we
say, "I'm your father. You do what I say." They feel it when they try to
make a choice and we say, "You have to clear everything with me, and
don't think otherwise." Sometimes we can communicate a feeling that
they are subject to our royal position by the way we talk to them about our
possessions. Instead of "This is our house" or "our yard," they hear, "This
is my house, my yard, my stuff."

Holding fast to a throne-room attitude builds a sense of detachment between the monarch-controllers and their children. Kids don't want to be subjects; they want to be sons and daughters. And this haughty attitude of the monarch-controller also causes a spouse to lose his or her sense of longing for the mate. The wisest parent and most loving partner takes Jesus' advice: *"Whoever wishes to become great among you shall be your servant"* (Matthew 20:26).

The Master: Her Loved Ones Feel Like Slaves

Without realizing it, individuals can develop a controlling style that resembles the relationship between masters and slaves. Every once in a while, I hear statements coming out of my mouth that make me a sound a lot like the master of the house. "Cody, get me the salt." "Karis, run back to my room and bring me my penny loafers." Does it sound innocent to you? I hope not, because it's not.

There's a wonderful word we can add to such statements that changes them from commands to requests. It's the word *please*. When my children want me to do something for them, they're expected to say please. And it goes both ways. If I want the salt, a noncontrolling way to ask is, "Cody, Daddy would like some seasoning for his eggs. Would you mind bringing me the salt, please?" And when he brings it to me, I should *thank* him. These may sound like common courtesies, but they're often abused or neglected within the home.

By turning my need from a command to a request, I let Cody know I recognize his individuality and also have a respect for what he's doing at the moment I ask.

My daughter Karis helps me by keeping my shoes shined. I get them done professionally at airports, so she doesn't have to do them often. But every once in a while, I call on her to buff them up. Now, suppose I were reading the newspaper at the kitchen table one evening and said to Karis, who was at the other end of the table doing her homework, "Honey, my penny loafers are in the bedroom and need to be polished for my trip tomorrow. Would you mind putting a shine on them for me?" I have placed my request before her. Suppose, however, she responds, "Daddy, I can do that, but it's really going to put me behind on my homework. This math assignment is tougher than I thought it would be. I'll do whatever you say. It's your call, Dad."

Is she being insubordinate? Some would say so, but I don't think she is. She's asking me to make a choice from the position that I hold as father. She's asking me to weigh which is more important, her homework or my shoes. Karis and I have a father-daughter relationship, not one of a master relating to a slave.

If she refuses me and I go shine them myself, I haven't let a child run my life. I've simply recognized the obvious; she has an agenda, too. If I want her to respect my agenda, I need to respect hers.

It may sound as if we're the Waltons. Trust me, we're far from it. Maybe I'm sensitive about mastering my kids because I could do it so easily. Like many parents, I could fall into the trap of treating them as though they're simply extensions of my eyes, ears, arms, and legs. They aren't. Neither is my wife. When we refuse to treat one another like slaves, we develop a sense of freedom within the family, freedom that's essential to a grace-based home.

The Mugger: His Loved Ones Feel Like Sacrifices

Without doubt, the most aggressive and most vicious way to control other people is by mugging them. This happens when we attack them to get them to do our will. It's the loudest, harshest, and most offensive form of control we could ever use. And in most homes, it is used regularly.

Muggers come out of nowhere, catch people off guard, get what they want, and have no regard for any damages inflicted. Let me give you some lines muggers commonly use as weapons.

"Just shut your face and do what I tell you!"

"You jerk! Who do you think you're dealing with?"

"Don't even think of bringing that loser into my house! What do you have for brains, anyway? Styrofoam?"

Ugly talk, isn't it? It makes me shudder just to write it. It violates me just to think of its being used on another person. It kills me inside to think how easily I could use it if I weren't careful.

We mug people when we're angry. We may be legitimately upset at them, and they may need to have some hard and honest things said to them. But when we mug them, we want them to comply for our sake, not

36

theirs. We want them to relieve our pain, even if we have to damage them in the process.

We mug people when we're tired. Probably more than any other single factor, fatigue can cause a conscientious individual to throw his priorities out the window and viciously mug those he loves. Fatigue clouds our reason and lowers our guard. When we're tired, we are often at the mercy of our flesh. But mugging someone just because we're fatigued can leave lifelong scars.

We mug people because we're exasperated with them. They may have pushed our patience to an all-time limit. (What two-year-old doesn't do that daily?) We don't care about the consequences to their spirits, because we subtly feel that they deserve it.

We mug people because we're scared. Like cornered animals, we get desperate. And in that condition, we often don't calculate what the result of our actions will be. We just want action, and we want it *now.*

Let's step back for a moment. Just about every relationship requires that we occasionally come down hard on issues. *What determines whether we use control or not is our motive. And what determines whether it's mugging or not is our method.*

Control by mugging manifests itself in several ways. Let's give these names that will enable us to pick them out in our lives and in the lives of those who control us.

1. The Meteor Controller

This is the person whose anger seemingly comes out of nowhere. Victims of this control never know when the controller's rage is going to start raining down on them, but they know from experience to always keep a sharp lookout. I've talked with wives who feel their husbands can intimidate them even when things are going well, because right in the midst of some of their finest, tenderest moments, these men can burst into a rage that leaves the women cowering. Like the Scud missiles in the Persian Gulf War, you never know what kind of payload is on board.

2. The Mordacious Controller

New word? Listen to this definition: "biting in style or manner—caustic."[5] I've been guilty of this. I want something badly enough that I'm willing to sacrifice someone else's dignity to get it. Mordacious muggers do that with a few carefully chosen words. "They are arbitrary and often arrogant in tone. When criticizing something you've said or done, they seem to attack not just the particular behavior, but you, and they do so in an accusing way. They are contemptuous of their victims, considering them to be inferior people who deserve to be bullied and disparaged."[6]

3. *The Mine-Field Controller*

The most vicious weapons of any war are the ones you can't see until it's too late. During the Vietnam conflict, many men came home without legs because they'd stepped on buried land mines. Most of them considered themselves fortunate just to have survived the explosion. Others lost arms, eyes, and ears simply because they were too close to someone else who'd stepped on one.

So, too, mine-field controllers not only harm the spirit of the person they're attacking, but also the spirits of others in close proximity. Children's hearts get wounded when one person they love very much viciously explodes and wounds another person they love equally.

Yes, the explosions of mine-field controllers may effectively control others for a while, and they may even get the kind of reaction they're looking for, but in the long run, the harm done is too high to calculate.

One of the most common forms of exploding is the tantrum. Tantrums are like "a revolver in the hands of a weakling."[7] These explosions create a greater backlash of hostility and aggression than any other form of control. They obstruct the victims' ability to reason, thereby keeping them from taking the critical first step in resolution of the situation. Tantrums keep them from coming to grips with the controller's frustration. Often the victims respond with their own explosions, and even more damage is done.

A mugger feels he can justify his actions. Here are some of the reasons he gives:

1. He has a strong sense of what he thinks is right.

2. He is driven by the need to prove himself.

3. He gets results from emotionally mugging another, albeit at the expense of the relationship.

4. He figures that his victims will cower as a result of the mugging, and ultimately he'll get what he wants.

There's no doubt that controlling others by mugging works. It also stinks! The capacity to emotionally mug others seems to be innate within the human heart. It only comes to the surface if we let it, and it gains effectiveness the more we use it. Obviously, those who use this method need to confess, repent, and apologize to those they've hurt.

It's also apparent that those who put up with this kind of control are merely positioning themselves for a major crisis. Nobody wants to be a sacrifice for another person's selfishness.

The Moralist: Her Loved Ones Feel They Have to Be Saints

The last style of aggressive control I want to mention is perhaps the most evil. This control comes clothed in such righteous garments that, although it's easy to spot, it's the toughest to combat. The Lord Jesus came to set people free. He wants, in addition, to allow His freedom to encompass an entire family.[8] A home can receive no greater blessing than to have the relationships within that home bathed in God's grace. But the controlling individual can gain no greater tool to leverage against another person than the indisputable will of God.

I recall watching an installment of ABC's "Nightline." Jim and Tammy Baker were appearing before the American people to answer questions (via Ted Koppel) that had been on everybody's mind. Koppel posed the first question; Mr. Baker dodged it by quoting Scripture. Koppel fired a second question. Baker used his superior knowledge of God's Word to avoid giving a direct answer once again.

That's when Koppel stopped to reset the ground rules. Paraphrasing his point, he said, "Rev. Baker, we all have a great reverence for the scriptures. The Scripture stands so high that we dare not question it. By using it to defend your actions, you make it impossible for us to disagree with you. Every time I ask you a question, you wrap yourself up in the Bible. I'm going to ask you not to use the scriptures as a shield to hide behind. You have done some things that people feel are extremely questionable. Don't clothe yourself in something holy to keep from answering these legitimate concerns."

In our Christian homes, we have a responsibility before God to create an atmosphere that gracefully attracts people to the Savior. Further, we have a mandate from Him to raise our children *"in the discipline and instruction of the Lord"* (Ephesians 6:4b). Our spiritual convictions should fuel our agendas. God's love should overwhelm all relationships. And we should stand by the truth of His Word regardless of the cost.

Sometimes God's desires are unpopular. And sometimes we have to enforce those desires, even though some within our families resist. It's easy, however, to slip over an extremely thin line and use the Lord to get what we selfishly want. It's tempting to use God's Word to muscle those we love through guilt, shame, and fear. The last thing God wants is for us to use Him just to get our own way. But the temptation to do it is forever present in Christian homes.

Maybe your child doesn't want to go to bed. He's defying you. You've tried everything. You're desperate. And then it slips out: "I don't think Jesus is very pleased with you."

You want your husband to ask his boss for a raise. He's not convinced he deserves it. And he's definitely reluctant to risk burning a bridge with his employer. He opens his lunch at his desk and sees the note you've scribbled on his napkin: "Honey, I'll be praying that God will give you the courage to confront your boss about that raise."

You come home driving a new van. It's what you've always wanted, but it's way out of your price league. You're already in debt, and the payments from this vehicle are going to do you in. Your wife comes out to hear who's honking a horn in her driveway. As you step out of the truck, you can see the look of fear in her eyes. "Listen, Sweetheart," you say, "I felt the Lord tugging at my heart every time I drove by the dealership. When I took this one for a test drive, I felt God clearly telling me that this is the car he wanted us to have. Just think of all the ways we can use it to help the youth group on their outings."

How do others defend themselves against this kind of onslaught without feeling they're defying the entire heavenly host? I call that last example "name-dropping." "I certainly don't want to mention any names, but...*Jesus* told me you'd better do such and such." Spouses and children have been gagged by overbearing name-droppers who feel they speak for the Holy Spirit.

Of all the ways we can exercise illegitimate authority in someone else's life, no method carries with it such eternally negative consequences as when we use God and His Word to get what we selfishly want.

The psalmist said: *"Let the words of my mouth and the meditation of my heart be acceptable in Thy sight, O Lord, my rock and my Redeemer"* (Psalm 19:14).

Desperate situations may call for desperate measures. But we must make sure we aren't selfishly controlling in the process—especially by using Jesus to smack people into submission to our wants. A pastor friend told me of an incident where his name-dropping method of control backfired on him.

He and his wife were celebrating Advent with their children by lighting a candle each night and sharing a special Christmas reading with them. They had three children, two of whom were identical twins.

Each night, the children had been taking turns lighting the candles. On this particular night, the honor fell to one of his nine-year-old twin daughters.

Her sister immediately protested, "It's not your turn. You did it last night. It's *my* turn."

"No, you lit it last night. It's my turn!"

"I did not light it last night, and you know it. Now give me the matches and let me have my turn!"

So they went, back and forth, each one claiming to be the rightful recipient of the honor of lighting the candle. The father remembered that a child who looked like both of them had lit the candle the night before, but he wasn't certain which one it was. Rather than trying to help them find the truth, he decided to hit them over the head with another form of truth. He said, "Now isn't this interesting. Here we are, trying to focus our attention on the birth of Jesus, the God who became a baby in order to bring peace on earth, and instead you two are arguing between yourselves."

He was right, but he was even more desperate. One of the twins chimed back, "Dad, this isn't about Jesus, it's about candles!"

Both girls appreciated the Nativity, and both loved the God who had once inhabited the manger. Each was just convinced it was her turn to light the candle and didn't want to be denied the honor. The daughter's comeback to his statement showed Dad that he was trying to shortcut the problem for the sake of convenience and was using Jesus to do his dirty work for him. What he really needed to do was either find out whose turn it was or appeal for compromise. That was a tougher route to go, but in this situation, it would have been a better example of how Jesus could actually bring peace on earth and goodwill to men (or sisters!).

Telling Yourself the Truth

When we treat the people we love as students, subjects, slaves, or sacrifices, or when we impose our selfish definition of what a saint should be, we rob their hearts of freedom. God wants the words that come from our mouths to be acceptable in His sight—but the larger problem is our hearts. They need to be changed. If we lecture as managers, decree as monarchs, demand as masters, destroy as muggers, or pontificate as name-droppers, we drive a wedge between us and the people we're controlling.

People who refuse to succumb to the temptation to aggressively control those around them, however, put themselves in the position of faith that is ultimately the most secure. It means getting out of the way and letting God do whatever He's going to do in the hearts of those we love. It's tough, but it's truth. And it's the kind of truth that will set us and our families free.

CHAPTER 5

The Passive Controller

Most people don't realize how powerful subtlety can be until they've experienced it at the hands of a passive controller. It's like a velvet-covered brick to the head or a fur-covered boot in the rear.

In the last chapter, we looked at the aggressive ways people get what they want. In this chapter, we want to focus on the hard-to-detect but easy-to-feel methods passive controllers use to get others to meet their desires.

Those who exercise passive control are often the last ones you'd suspect. Sometimes they appear to be the victims of aggressive controllers. Few would suspect that these quiet people can manipulate with ease and know how to bring aggressive controllers to their knees. Their methods are utilized not just to counter other high controllers; they also take on the innocent—the people within their families who love and trust them. Because their methods are passive, it's hard to see them as culprits. And distinct from aggressive controllers, they don't always realize they're stepping over the boundaries of other people's lives.

Let's check out the paintings in this rogues' gallery. I need to warn you, though, that some of them are etched on mirrors. You may see yourself as you never have before.

The Masked Controller

Trick or treat! That had been the theme of Jerry and Marie's romance from the beginning. Marie wanted to marry Jerry. Jerry was almost ready to take the relationship to the final step and buy the ring, but before he did, he wanted a few more weeks to think about it. He'd been close to the altar once before and got burned. While the experience hadn't destroyed him, it had made him understandably cautious.

He'd been dating Marie for almost a year and really enjoyed her company. She seemed to embody a lot of the attributes he was looking for in a partner.

Marie, on the other hand, wasn't willing to risk the relationship, not even to the truth. She thought it might be better if he didn't know certain things about her until after the wedding. She reasoned his commitment to the marriage would be strong. After the wedding, when he found out about her shortcomings and secrets, he probably wouldn't say or do anything to end the relationship. She wasn't sure what he would do if he knew now. That's why she wore so many masks during their courtship.

One of the things she didn't tell him was that she smoked. She was amazed at how well she had concealed it. His feelings about smoking were clear, and she was certain he'd never agree to the marriage if he knew.

She told him that everything was great between herself and her parents, but in truth, things were not even good. Her father had been too familiar with her when she first blossomed at puberty. The second time it happened, she stood up to him, and he backed away. But the damage was done. Since that time, you could have driven an eighteen-wheeler between their hearts. She knew that sometimes a traumatic event like this could cause difficulty in the victim's ability to respond sexually. She wasn't sure if this would be true in her case, but just in case, she felt it best to keep the information from Jerry and wait to see if there would be a problem.

There was one final thing about Marie that Jerry didn't know—namely, that she had made a serious attempt at suicide in her early twenties. Afterward, she had spent two months in a rehabilitation center and a year in therapy. She was hoping the depression she'd experienced was now a thing of the past, but she suspected she hadn't completely licked it yet, because she had such a fear of its returning. She was too ashamed to tell Jerry she'd tried to kill herself, so she decided she'd just go on with life. She would continue the laughter, the smiles, and the masquerade.

I met Jerry and Marie several years and a couple of children after the wedding. Time had stripped away all of Marie's masks, but instead of dealing with her problems, she had replaced them with new ones. Now she manipulated in whatever way necessary to get Jerry to cooperate with her wishes. She had become a passive controller.

By wearing masks, however, she was still able to keep others at a safe distance. She could prevent them from snooping into her life. In so doing, she was a classic passive controller, insuring that others would deal with her the way she chose.

This is how it works: A husband says his finances are better than they are to keep his wife from discovering his gambling problem. A daughter feigns interest in her parents' hobbies to get them to buy her something she really wants.

There's nothing new about wearing masks. We've been doing it since sin entered the world. Blatant transparency is frightening. It leaves us too vulnerable. But at the same time, opaque, masked relationships aren't fair. They rob the people we love. Because some people fear the unknown so much, they have perfected the wearing of masks to such a level that they don't always realize they're doing it. But if we love others, our commitment should lead us to openness and oneness with them.

Had Marie been honest with Jerry, she would have been surprised by his response. His love for her was greater than the disappointments of her past or her struggles in the present. The years of wearing masks to keep from being vulnerable had shut down openness between them and turned her into a mystery. By the time they sought help, Jerry's trust in her had been seriously eroded.

Hiding behind a mask might protect our vulnerabilities, but at the same time it makes deceivers of us. Our hiding misleads children who need to be able to trust us. It misrepresents marital vows that were founded on mutual confidence. It misappropriates the truth in our friendships and business commitments.

Most people who live behind masks don't realize the potential jeopardy in which they put their emotions. On the one hand, masks can be worn so effectively that the wearers actually start believing the illusions they're trying to foist on others. On the other hand, life has a bad habit of testing the true colors of our character. Eventually, circumstances come along that tear off our masks, destroy our illusions, and leave us at the mercy of the people we've been manipulating for years. It is, indeed, a fragile position to be in. That's when we discover that what people didn't know about us hurts them far more than what they did know.

Masked control. Hide and seek becomes a damaging form of passive control. But the next kind of control is just as dangerous.

The Miser Controller

All of us have basic needs that were built into us by God. We need food, clothing, shelter, safety, and affection. Some individuals seem to need more than the basics, however. For them, the list is nearly endless. When we have needs that others must fulfill, we give them a tool to leverage against our wishes. That's what makes relationships so risky.

Years ago, while attending graduate school, I met Charles. He was a "bootstrap" businessman who had built his insurance company from a few clients up to thousands. He had moved his office from a small room in his garage to a downtown skyscraper.

Everybody loved Charles. He had a gentle demeanor, and his spiritual convictions ran deep. As a father, his early track record would have qualified him for an award. Because he didn't have a lot of money in his early years, he and his wife, Sarah, didn't have the option of overindulging their children. Yet looking back, they all admit that the happy years of their family life had been the "hungry years."

Charles was more than prudent as a businessman; he was also shrewd. The principles he followed were as biblical and above reproach as anyone could find. That's why he had gained so many clients so quickly. By the time the kids were in high school, Charles was well on his way to becoming a multimillionaire.

But before he ever had a thousand dollars in the bank, he'd figured out how to manipulate people with his money. He'd also learned the tremendous power it gave him to control his family. No member of his family ever got a dime from him without an explanation of how hard it had been for him to earn it. His gifts came with strings attached. To maintain complete control, he made the family clear all of their expenditures with him. Strangely enough, at times he would encourage them to be frivolous with money, at the same time reminding them who had given it to them to enjoy.

People outside the family would have called Charles generous, but he didn't really fit the definition. Inside his head were file drawers where he maintained careful accounts of the dollars he had invested in the people around him. Don't get me wrong; Charles gave a lot of money to his wife, his children, and a host of charities. But he wasn't generous. Generous people consider it a privilege to share, a joy to give, and they don't attach strings to the money they give. Charles's money had more than strings attached—it had chains welded to it. So, in reality, Charles never actually *gave* his money away. He simply moved it from an interest-bearing account at the bank to the accounts of others, and the interest he demanded from them was loyalty, devotion, and obedience.

I watched what this control did to his children. Through their teenage years, they became more and more financially dependent on him. They all went to work for him except for one son who refused to be bought. Charles disenfranchised him and banned him from the family circle. To this day, his brothers and sister are afraid to socialize with him for fear of retribution from their father.

Charles took title to the lives of those children who went to work for him. Now, without demanding a single thing, he can get them to do whatever he wants. When it came to choosing a husband, his daughter fell directly in line with Charles's wishes. He waited for her to bring home a guy who met his two criteria. First, he wanted someone who would be good to his daughter. Second, he wanted someone he could control. When she found the right candidate, Charles threw his money and his blessing at them in one fell swoop.

Unless you got real close to this family and were looking for it, you would never realize how effectively Charles ran them with his money. But they knew, and they felt powerless to do anything about it.

Misers horde anything they know someone else needs. They may seem to be meeting the needs of those around them, but if you look closely, there are expectations attached. Some hold out hoops and make those around them jump through before they will move to meet their needs. Parents withhold love and affection from their children as a means of controlling them. Miser kids withhold affection when they're frustrated with their parents and dish it out when they want something. Moms horde resources, dads horde time, and men horde authority.

Eight zillion years ago, women discovered they could use sex to get what they wanted. By defrauding their husbands, withholding sex, or, at the other extreme, devouring them, they could get them to cooperate with their selfish agendas. So, miser-controller women horde sex or dole it out as needed.

Most partners know when sex is being used to manipulate or coerce, but they allow the manipulation to happen because their need for it overrides their sense of being used.

Misers leverage unbelievable control on a relationship. They also create unbelievable disappointment. Few people can live at the whims of a miser without experiencing serious wounds to their spirits.

The Magnifying Controller

My kids, like 100 percent of the other children in the world, love balloons. I know they've stopped by McDonald's at the mall when I come home from work in the evening to find a half dozen rubber spheres floating at different altitudes throughout the house. One of the great wake-up calls of my life happened when I got up in the middle of the night to check on one of the kids and accidentally stepped on a medium-sized balloon that had drifted into the bedroom. It exploded, and I thought my wife, Darcy, was going to have to jump-start my heart!

Balloons are great illustrations of our third type of passive controller—the magnifier. A noninflated balloon doesn't pose much of a presence.

You can write a message on it in script so tiny that you have to squint to read it. But inflate the balloon and the message expands until it's clearly readable. Filled with helium, the balloon takes on a life of its own, bouncing here and there.

Magnifying controllers use balloon principles to manipulate circumstances. They take some small, insignificant thing and blow it all out of proportion, just in time to change an outcome. That's what magnifying control is all about—affecting outcomes. Children often do not feel the freedom—or have the verbal ability—to joust with their parents on a particular issue. Parents know that and can use it. They realize that by overdramatizing, overemphasizing, or overanalyzing an issue, they can turn children from one way of looking at something to another.

Most people who magnify an issue are not aware they're doing it. They genuinely believe the problem they're focusing on is bigger than it is. By blowing up the issue, they can stall a decision that they don't look forward to making. "This works, because as life proceeds, most decisions, if unmade, quickly become irrelevant," says Robert M. Bramson.[1]

I recall a woman whose husband was asked to move across the country to take a key position with his company. It was a prime opportunity to make a quantum leap both professionally and financially. This was also the only promotion the company had to offer at the time. As the wife contemplated all the trauma that would be involved in uprooting, moving, and putting down stakes again, her insecurities came to the forefront. The husband knew it would be difficult to move as well. (In emotional stress tests, moving cross-country is right up there with burying a loved one.)

The wife had a legitimate basis for her concerns, but she didn't have a legitimate basis for the extreme analysis she brought to every decision. The mere listing of their home with a real estate agent became an impossible task. First, she interviewed a number of realtors and was never satisfied. Then she demanded two additional appraisals because she refused to accept the first. To further complicate things, she limited the showing of the house to only one afternoon a week because she said she had too many details to tend to. "I just can't keep the house looking as it should," she said. She maintained this pattern throughout the process of attempting to sell the house.

Meanwhile, rather than downsizing her church activities in preparation for their move, she became involved in a number of new projects—projects that would require her being around for a long time.

Her husband tried commuting—two weeks back East, one weekend home. That got old quickly. When he tried to speed up the process of selling the house, his wife pulled out her stack of detailed notes on why it wasn't as easy as he thought. When they got an offer that was decent but lower than their asking price, he wanted to accept it, but she refused to budge. She gave an elaborate response about their not having all the money they would need when they moved if they took the lesser offer. Ultimately she got what she wanted: He gave up the promotion and eventually resigned from the company. This woman didn't want to disrupt her life, regardless of how it affected those around her. In the end, the entire family paid the price.

Magnifiers can control with a handful of expressions:

"Yes, but . . . "

"However . . . "

"You didn't consider that . . . "

"It's not that simple."

They tend to be people who are detail oriented, can't stand change, are intimidated by risks, and don't like to make decisions where someone has to go through discomfort. Interestingly, they usually marry visionaries and dreamers.

The Marshmallow Controller

Some of the nicest people I know are some of the most effective passive controllers. They're sensitive, sweet, compassionate, loyal, and as under-standing as anyone could be. But they can play a situation to their liking by simply refusing to do *anything*. These people won't take a stand, confront, argue, or even defend themselves. They passively control the people that love them by being marshmallows. When you're married to one of these, you think you're living with an echo. ("Whatever you say, Honey. It's up to you.")

These people are driven by their overwhelming need to be liked and accepted. That's why they're so kind to the people around them. But when life spits nails at them and challenges the relationships they treasure, they tend to turn into putty and take no stand. When they're confronted with a

50

situation where something needs to be done and they either don't want to do it or don't have the capabilities, rather than risk the relationship, they will simply agree. Later on, they don't follow through.[2]

Marshmallow controllers protect their areas of insecurity by doing nothing and then forcing others to pick up the slack. The end result is that the people close to them have to take more responsibility for them than they should. And from the safety of their nonaggressive posture, marshmallows protect themselves from being hurt or hurting anyone else. They are emotionally lazy. They'd much rather ride on another person's strengths. And when all is said and done, they get what they wanted all along—a free relational ride.

What a shame! Their innocuous nature is a liability to those they love, because they avoid the hard parts of relationships that bring out the best in each of us.

The Monopolizing Controller

Sometime back, I was involved in a marriage conference at which I heard a couple arguing. The discussion was about their son who was just starting his freshman year of high school. The father wanted to take him on a trip to visit three military academies as well as a few Ivy League universities. The wife was adamant that she wasn't going to let him lure her "baby" away from their home in southern California. She wasn't going to allow him to be exposed to all that "high brow" snobbery. She forbade him from even mentioning his idea to her son. "I'll not have it. That's *my* son."

"That's *our* son," he fired back.

She turned, stared him dead square in the eyes, and said, "As long as I'm alive, he's *my* son."

This father had landed on Boardwalk, and she wasn't even giving him the opportunity to come up with the rent. Her monopoly on the soul of her son let her husband know that as far as she was concerned, he could go directly to jail, not pass Go, and not collect $200.

Like this woman, most of us have the bad habit of putting the personal pronoun *my* in front of the key parts of our lives—my house, my car, my clothes, my spouse, my kids. This sense of ownership is one of the most subtle but effective forms of passive control.

Children find it difficult to have a sense of individuality when they feel

51

they are only someone's personal and private possession. Teasing a spouse about being a "love slave" is only humorous if he or she is *not*. When people take ownership of those close to them, it's easy to begin manipulating in order to gain their selfish desires.

A word that names what we've been describing is *attachment*. Two good synonyms for attachment are *ownership* and *possessiveness*. Attachment doesn't work. What does work is detachment, and healthy love strives to achieve it. Detachment moves us toward control-free relationships. This is the best attitude to maintain toward all the skills, resources, and opportunities God places in our lives. This attitude maintains a stance that God owns all we have; we are merely stewards for Him. This is God's job, God's car, God's child, God's man or woman. By encouraging this attitude, we become givers rather than takers in a relationship.

Most people who control by monopolizing the people and resources around them do it without having any personal, internal conflict. It's subtle. It's powerful. And it's emotionally devastating to the people they possess.

The Microphone Controller

Another group of controllers are those who simply dominate conversations. This is what I call the "microphone method" of overcontrol. Microphone controllers utilize superior verbal skills to keep others from expressing an opinion. They control by being the only ones who get to verbalize a position. I've observed numerous marriages where this is a problem.

The beginnings of this kind of control are usually found in the original matchup of the partners. A quiet, unassuming individual marries an articulate, confident, and often opinionated partner. It looks as if it could be a match made in heaven. Surely they can fill the gaps in each other's makeup and enjoy a fantastic life together.

For some the marriage does just that, but for others, it's something else entirely. If one person wants to manipulate the relationship, he simply seizes the verbal higher ground. He not only dominates the conversation, but he also monopolizes the philosophy, goals, and dreams of his partner and all those around him. Should someone of lesser verbal skills articulate anything contrary to his wishes, he will humiliate that person into submission with cutting criticism. A spouse or child knows when he's outgunned, and rather than fight, he'll comply in order to avoid conflict.

When I was in college, a certain young man stood out in my conservative circles for his staunch support of liberal, sometimes extremely militant, political causes. He was an antithesis to his family. After getting to know him, I discovered why. His father was a pastor with a big chip on his shoulder. He was an angry man with a Bible and a big mouth.

Throughout the 1960s, this pastor held to such a strict "Americanized gospel" that to listen to him, one would think Jesus had been born in Bethlehem, Pennsylvania, and then slept in the Lincoln bedroom at the White House until He began His public ministry. The preacher preached his folly not only from the pulpit, but also from the dining room table. However, too many things were happening in, to, and because of the United States in the 1960s. Those events made his sermons sound ridiculous. His son (my classmate) thought his father was naive and misguided.

Saying so cost him plenty. Not only did his father verbally remove his son's head at home, but the next Sunday, he also made him the butt of his angry sermon at church. In that house, there was no such thing as dialogue. That would require the free exchange of ideas and feelings between two people. There was only a monologue with an audience that applauded faithfully. As far as I know, my classmate is still carrying his membership card in the liberal left—a position not of ideology but of desperation.

Microphone controllers devalue people. Our opinions, like our faces, names, and reputations, are precious to us. When we sense that someone is deliberately manipulating our ideas or strong-arming our ideals, we feel cheapened. And when the voice hogging the microphone is charming, love and life can get extremely confusing.

The Monastic Controller

In real life, monastics are those who lead lives of silence and withdrawal. But some passive controllers embrace this exclusive style in order to control others. Deep within the monastic controller's heart lies a powerful weapon to use against contrary opinions: *silence*. The meek may inherit the earth, but silent controllers can run your life. Without firing a shot, they can pierce your resolve. Without saying a thing, they can take the words right out of your mouth.

Dialogue is a family treasure—the gold and silver that finances our hopes and underwrites our dreams. It may draw laughter, tears, or anger, but when tempered with grace, it gives individuals a sense of high value. When people verbally and/or physically withdraw from the mainstream of relationships, however, they can control the people close to them. By building invisible walls around themselves, they put others off-balance enough to manipulate them.

You've heard the expression "an argument from silence." It refers to the overwhelming point that is made by what is *not* said. Those who control with silence defraud those who need two sides of a conversation to feel they've been heard. Silence can communicate disapproval. Withdrawal can communicate shame. The withholding of affection can communicate disdain. And all these tactics can be used to coerce loved ones into complying with the monastic controllers' wishes in the hope they'll get their needs met.

When parents withdraw affection and dialogue from their children, it makes them feel helpless. When a spouse dishes out the "silent treatment," he or she moves the partner to a state of exasperation. Manipulating for selfish reasons is easy at that point. In most cases, a spouse will do anything to draw a mate out of self-imposed isolation. It isn't surprising that resentment builds in this type of passive but high-control environment.

The Mirage Maker

There are three reasons you don't want to live in Phoenix. They are June, July, and August. Other than those, it's a beautiful place to raise a family. Our state is famous for a lot of things, but it is notorious for two— our heat and our politics. My observation is that one is responsible for the other. When you're traveling either by foot or car across the desert, the light can play tricks on your eyes. Looking into the distance, you might notice the sunlight shimmering off a lake that isn't there. This phenomenon, of course, is known as a mirage. It's caused by the bending or reflecting of rays of light through varying densities of heated air.

High-control individuals can manipulate families into creating mirages—showing the world relationships that aren't there. These mirages become essential parts of their distorted view of security. Or they may create the mirages within the family itself and fake out the people who are supposed to have access to truth within relationships.

Whether it's done to the people on the inside looking out or to those on the outside looking in, it's a destructive form of passive control. It gives the *appearance* that things are great, healthy, cheerful, or peaceful. But these situations often hide the worst types of abuse—physical, emotional, sexual, or criminal.

Leaders of families with this blatant form of control work overtime to present an image that says, "Everything's fine." It's not uncommon in this type of home for a heavy emphasis to be put on looks, beauty, physical prowess, excellence in sports, academic achievement, or high moral or spiritual endeavors. That's why, when you hear of some horrible event within a family, the neighbors, interviewed by the press, often say things like, "They seemed to be such a close and happy family" or "He seemed like such an easygoing kid." When the pathological studies are done, however, you often find that the child was living in a high-control pressure cooker with no release valve. These are the kinds of homes where mirage control does the most damage.

In these "Appearance is everything" homes, a child might be struggling from the friction between his parents, but he's forbidden to mention anything to relatives or teachers who could offer him emotional support while his parents work out their differences. Or a family might be experiencing a series of financial setbacks, but their daughter is forbidden from mentioning anything to her Sunday school teacher who might be able to give her spiritual encouragement. The parents are trying to avoid embarrassment or having to answer sensitive questions, but often at innocent family members' expense. Because the parents are as victimized by their insecurities as their children, they are often incapable of supporting their children.

Pride causes families to create mirages through the unwilling or unwitting cooperation of their own members. What we don't realize when we're creating mirages is that they only work from a distance. When people get close enough, they will see us for what we are.

Numbers 32:23 says, *"Be sure your sin will find you out."* That's a good reminder for passive controllers who think that creating illusions will ultimately work. Homes of honor have nothing to hide. Homes of truth have nothing to lose.

The methods of passive control can be harsh and hard to detect or soft and subtle, but the effect is the same. Most people lean to the method that most aligns with their personality strength. But there's one more style of control that is generally developed out of a state of desperation. It brings the worst of passive control and aggressive control together to form a powerful persuasion. In our next chapter, we'll take a close look at the most frustrating form of an overcontroller—the passive/aggressive.

CHAPTER 6

The Passive/Aggressive Controller

A proud, Irish family farmed some land a couple of miles from my childhood home in western Pennsylvania. Their son, Bobby, attended grade school with me. He had a deportment track record that made just about everything I did look good. That's because he consistently upstaged me when it came to getting into trouble with the teacher.

Miss Carrick, the woman assigned to the third year of our academic career, had a practice of posting our criminal records on the blackboard. If you crossed one of her many behavioral lines, your name went on the board, and with it all the embarrassment and shame of being an elementary school misfit. If you got a paddling, your name went to the top of the list and couldn't be erased for seven days. Bobby had such a difficult time adjusting to Miss Carrick's arbitrary standards that he generally held the pole position on the list of offenders.

One weekend, Bobby's dad took him and his two sisters for a hike in the woods behind their acreage. His father prided himself on his demeanor with wild animals and naively assumed that all God's creatures are friendly if treated properly. That's what gave him the dumb idea to demonstrate to his kids how he could get a skunk to eat cookies directly from his hand.

His little demonstration backfired. Everyone got nailed. Bobby and his sisters missed several days of school as a result. They took enough tomato juice baths to cause their skin to break out. But sometimes there's mercy in humiliation. For an entire week, Bobby's name stayed off the blackboard, and all because his father dared mess with an animal that controls with a pungent and effective method of passive/aggressive behavior.

Passive/aggressive control is a nightmarish combination of the two forms of control we've already explored. Passive/aggressive controllers have the "in your face" potential of the aggressive controller, but their aggression is housed in the meek and often innocent-looking mask of a passive controller. Like passive controllers, they can pull strings in your life without your being able to figure out how it's happening.

Passive/aggressive control is common among children and teenagers. Since they don't feel old enough, big enough, or smart enough to win full-scale battles against the wills of their parents, they try to beat them down through calculated ambushes on their sanity. High-control kids are the Stonewall Jacksons of the home.

Stonewall Jackson was one of the most-feared Confederate generals of the Civil War. He was feared because of his deadly ambushes on Northern troops. Rather than engage the enemy in full-scale, frontal war on a battlefield spread out over many miles, Jackson preferred to "float and sting." He was notorious for appearing out of nowhere, striking the Northern army in its most vulnerable position, inflicting heavy casualties, and then disappearing before the enemy could pursue.

Jackson's effectiveness came as much from the intimidation the enemy felt—from the way the North just *knew* he was out there somewhere—as it did from his actual exploits. Often, he had the foe so emotionally defeated that all he had to do was *appear* and the outcome of the battle became academic.

Kids can operate on the same principle. They rattle their parents' cages, overwhelming them without having to actually engage them in a strength-against-strength conflict. How much do I love to control thee, let me count the ways. Kids control by:

- being consistently late
- being forgetful

- being undemonstrative
- letting their grades drop
- refusing to keep their hair nice
- always wearing black
- withdrawing
- leaving the gas tank empty
- doing "innocent" things that embarrass their parents in public
- hanging around unambitious friends
- dating "questionable" people

Kids use passive/aggressive behavior (e.g., lower grades) to evoke an aggressive reaction from their parents. Though they aren't blatantly antagonistic, they drive their parents crazy nonetheless. They can manipulate parents into either backing off or complying with certain desires, simply by using quiet defiance. It's the "I may be sitting down on the outside, but I'm standing up on the inside" mind-set.

High-Octane Control

Passive/aggressive behavior is mostly displaced anger with a lot of denial mixed in. Those are the therapeutic terms we use to define the phenomenon. Passive/aggressive people are extremely exasperated individuals—almost desperate. Their anger usually stems from a series of blocked expectations that give them no avenue for ventilating their frustration. And one other thing characterizes this form of control: It's generally turned inward, thereby hurting the controllers as much as the people they're trying to control.

The controller who lets his grades take a nosedive may light a perfectionist mother's fuse, but in the end, it's him who flunks out of school. Being late for everything may have the intended effect on an overbearing father, but in the end, it's still the controller who's late.

A more self-destructive form of passive/aggressive behavior is eating disorders. Two disorders with disastrous effects are anorexia, a diet gone mad in which the victim is literally starving herself to death; and bulimia, binge eating and purging. When a member of a family has an eating disorder, the entire family is affected. The person's behavior holds the spirit of the family in chains while threatening her own life.

Dealing with someone who has an eating disorder is frustrating. It seems impossible to isolate the cause(s). For the disorder to be maintained, the person must be a card-carrying controller. He or she uses passive/aggressive behavior on the outside to hide the eating disorder inside. Denial abounds in these situations and surrounds the key people involved. Even the person with the disorder is hard pressed to articulate the causes behind her behavior, because she doesn't know either.

What happens when passive/aggressive children become adults? They simply cultivate their crude methods of control into an art form. Marriage partners and parents can be some of the biggest users and abusers of passive/aggressive techniques. Usually these are the people who feel powerless. They don't have (or don't *think* they have) a way to change the people and circumstances around them.

A passive/aggressive person may be married to a control czar who refuses to take into account that person's best interests. Out of desperation, the passive/aggressive individual throws into motion behavioral patterns that drive the partner up the proverbial wall.

Headaches, chronic tardiness, not getting the house cleaned, not getting home from work on time, burning dinner, overeating—it's an endless list of listless ends—the visible evidence of backwashed bitterness.

Underground Emotions

Emotions go "clandestine" out of desperation. They are driven down and hidden beneath the surface of day-to-day relationships because of the hard lesson learned the last time they went public. The result is passive/aggressive behavior.

A wife may be passive/aggressive because she lived in a home where her father removed her dignity with harsh words, her confidence with put-downs, and her hopes with criticism. She may be married to a man who is the antithesis of her father, but early formatting and fear hold her in the control patterns she learned as a child. She "submarines" people around her, refusing to surface her emotions and deal heart to heart with the people she loves.

A husband may have been publicly and financially emasculated by a first wife, so he becomes passive/aggressive with his second wife and unwittingly punishes her for the sins of her predecessor.

Life and love shouldn't be so complicated, but when they're played out in high-control relationships, they are. At no place is this seen more clearly than in the way people control through passive/aggressive behavior. I've provided a laundry list of some of the obvious ways kids, parents, and partners use this tool. But before we conclude this chapter, I want to look at a few of the other ways passive/aggressive behavior plays itself out in relationships.

The Moaner

Do you ever feel like Moses leading the children of Israel in a bunch of circles in the wilderness? The bickering, whining, and complaining that come from many of the back rooms of our houses can rise like a cloud and hover for days at a time. To a certain extent, moaning is to be expected within the family. Some conditions almost always produce it: stress, hunger, confusion, and fatigue are a few. Normally, we can take into consideration these conditions that family members might be feeling and come up with a fairly tolerant attitude toward the complainer.

But some people use moaning and complaining as a tool to manipulate the people around them. It's not done in an outwardly aggressive way, but it works as well as if it had been. There are several reasons some people use this form of control:

1. Complainers point out real problems, but they do it in a manner that elicits placating or defensive responses from others. The complainers' frustration at the lack of constructive problem solving is genuine but self-defeating, since it only leads to more complaining.

2. Complaining may be the only kind of active behavior that seems possible to those who feel powerless in determining their own fate. They believe everything that happens to them is attributable to the benevolent or malevolent actions of others.

3. Complainers have strong ideas about how others ought to behave.

They feel genuine—if sometimes disguised—anger when those others don't conform to their wishes.

4. Complaining becomes self-validating, because it provides a solid basis for complainers to confirm their own lack of responsibility for anything not done well. They continue to feel personally "perfect."[1]

What distinguishes moaners from people with legitimate complaints is that moaners aren't problem solvers; they're just problem identifiers. It's their way of processing emotional frustration. They come off as "wet blankets." By being consistently negative, they can get more powerful people than themselves to take action on their behalf. It's obvious why kids revert to this method of control. It works! But having found it so useful in childhood, many of them carry the habit into adult life.

The Mood Controller

A family I know tolerated an adult mood controller longer than they should have. But since he presided as the sole head of their home, they didn't feel they had many options. Matthew was a hardworking, conscientious father of four who loved his kids and brought a lot of good intentions to his responsibilities as family leader. His wife had left him with all the children a couple of years after their last child was born.

Matthew seldom lashed out at people who frustrated him. That was part of the reason he ended up divorced. In addition, he was moody and would hold his kids' emotions in limbo with his unpredictable mood swings. If he was happy, everyone was supposed to be happy. If he was sad, he didn't appreciate the children's enjoying themselves. And should he come home in a foul mood, it was better that the kids keep their distance. He never turned his anger on them, but he made it clear he didn't need their help in solving his problems.

It's a shame his kids didn't feel confident enough to confront him with his behavior years earlier than they finally did. But without another parent to help them, they simply didn't think it was their place. Several years after the divorce, one child finally mustered the courage to speak honestly with him, and as a result, Matthew started taking responsibility for the effect his moods had on others. Once confronted, he admitted his moods gave him a sense of control in an otherwise out-of-control life.

Matthew carried a heavier cross than most, but his overwhelming moods weren't the way to lighten it. Fortunately for him and his children, he had a commitment to the Lord and to them that enabled him to see his moods for what they were—an illegitimate way to cope.

Don't misunderstand. Matthew's emotions were legitimate. When he was genuinely angry, sad, or frustrated, he needed to have an outlet to express those emotions. The problem was that he expected the rest of the family to submit to his emotional shifts regardless of their own needs. Those expectations moved him from being an emoter to becoming a controller.

There's room for moods in families. The key is recognizing when they're true expressions of the heart and when they're just muscle being exercised against others. When they're the latter, it's time to call the pattern control and help the offender deal with it.

The Mafia

One of my closest friends is a man named Joe Carlo. If I were to die, I'd want him to be one of my pallbearers. He's given me an advanced education about the way teenage boys develop emotionally. He had three simultaneously. During the time they were teens, I was working with the youth group at his church. Joe and his wife, Judy, were tremendous parents who gave their three sons what I like to call a "legacy of love."

My wife, Darcy, and I were at the reception for their oldest son's wedding. We had a ball. Joe was the perfect patriarch and looked distinguished in his tailored tuxedo. Now, you might recognize that Joe's last name has an ethnic ring to it. Joe is Italian, and in his tuxedo, he greatly resembled many of the characters in the gangster movies that give those of Italian descent such an unfair stereotype. But Joe handles all of Hollywood's mistakes in good humor and even makes fun of himself in the process.

Most of the guests had gone, and the crew was starting to clean up. Joe, tired from all the festivities, had settled in a chair in the middle of the ballroom. Flanked by his two younger sons (looking the part in their tuxedos), he was carrying on some light banter. The two violinists who had been serenading the crowd throughout the evening were walking by me to put their instruments away and head home. I couldn't resist the opportunity. I asked if they had one more song left in them and then whispered what I wanted to hear. It turned out perfectly.

They walked slowly toward Joe and, on cue, started playing the haunting theme of *The Godfather*. Joe loved it. He went right into his impression of Marlon Brando doing Don Corleone. I was dying with laughter as he talked about how "Tessio sleeps with the fishes."

This was a great moment with a great friend. I enjoyed it so much because if Joe is anything, he's a father who has done his parenting from a position of grace. And he has three fine sons to show for his efforts.

I wish more families were like his. But, unfortunately, what he was pretending when playing the godfather is just too real in many homes. Parents, both fathers and mothers, can subtly develop a network of allegiances that play one child against another, or a group of children against a spouse. They assume a role as "godfather" over their families and expect certain members to maintain blind loyalty regardless of what the scenario is. It's a system of use and abuse in which one person assumes the right to exact favors from people close to him without their having a right to ask questions. When a couple is struggling in their relationship, one or the other can pull certain of the children into "syndication."

Rather than behave aggressively toward the people they desire to control, mafia controllers simply outgun the other parent by enlisting the children to take up their cause. Without having to face off directly, these manipulators still get the desired response. And in the process, the children are guided into doing the dirty work between two people who can't seem to communicate honestly. Obviously, "mafias" can develop easily in families divided by divorce.

"Godfathers" offer deals that family members can't refuse, but sometimes their deals develop into feuds that carry on for decades.

The Martyr Controller

I was flying from Nashville to Los Angeles on a flight that would get me into my hotel about 2:00 A.M. It had been a long and somewhat discouraging day of work, and I was badly in need of sleep. I was hoping to get some rest on the last leg of the journey from Dallas to the City of Angels. It seems, however, that the only reason you make plans is so someone else can have the joy of breaking them.

Since there was just a handful of passengers on board, the flight attendants had time to visit with us during the meal service. As they served mine, they asked what I do for a living. Describing myself as an "advocate for the family" apparently piqued their interest. When they were done with their work, two of them, a man and a woman, came back to talk to me. They knelt facing backward in the seats in front of me. That way we could talk face to face. The male attendant wanted some advice, and the female attendant wanted to hear what I had to say.

He was in love with a girl he desperately wanted to marry, he said. The feeling was mutual. The girl was ready to accept his proposal as soon as he was ready to give it.

"What's holding you back?" I asked.

His response was classic. He was the youngest of three sons—the baby. His mother was a widow. The older brothers were already married with families. Except for the years that he'd gone away to college, he'd lived at home. His father had died shortly after he graduated from college. Because she feared being alone, and because she was not adjusting well to widowhood, his mother clung to him. She began to remind him frequently of her many sacrifices on his behalf.

He hadn't dated many girls since he started his career as a flight attendant, but she treated those he had with cold indifference. Now that he seemed to be genuinely in love, his mother had increased her martyr control by making him feel guilty for even considering leaving her alone.

"All I ever did was care for you when you needed me," she'd tell him. "I feel discarded." It was one of her worn-out lines. I told him I'd seen his story in several old movies. He knew his situation wasn't unique; he simply didn't know how to deal with his mother. The guilt was overriding.

Bless her heart. It's frightening to be alone. When your whole life has revolved around a husband and three sons and you suddenly find yourself facing an empty house, the reality of your aloneness can cloud your reasoning. It can make you actually think there is not and never will be anyone out there to fill the void. Loneliness is one of the worst companions of the widowed, the elderly, and the infirm.

In this case, the man's mother was neither feeble nor immobile. She was just scared and somewhat selfish. Her martyr attitude was putting a noose around her son's capacity to love and strangling the life out of it.

I was curious and so took a shot in the dark. "This really isn't new, is it?" I said. "She's used this martyr complex on you since you were a little kid, hasn't she?"

He thought about it a few minutes and then started nodding his head. "Come to think of it, she has. She's used it on all of us, including my dad. How did you know?"

"Trust me, it was a lucky guess. I'm usually wrong more than I'm right." We went on to discuss passive/aggressive control and how she had perfected it as a style of manipulating him since he was a child. And although she had no malicious intentions, her control was still having a destructive effect on his life. We then talked about "honest love." He began thinking out loud of a legitimate plan that could minimize her concerns, while at the same time let him get on with his life.

Martyrs traffic in guilt. They play on the sympathies of their victims in ways that few others can. Those who use the martyr form of passive/aggressive control are tapping into the same emotions the passive miser uses. Instead of hoarding resources, martyrs give sacrificially; but each "loving deed" for family members becomes a "marker" they can call in some time in the future.

Martyrdom is quite effective, but it's not kind. I've caught myself using it to remind my children of how much I've given to make their life good, comfortable, or significant. When I do this, I turn a loving act of parenting into an act from which I can exact a toll. When I see martyr control in my life, I try to respond by calling it what it is—wicked. When I play the martyr, it puts my children in a beholding position to me. Healthy family relationships are held together not by guilt but by grace. And when I do something kind or generous for my family, I shouldn't do it with a martyr's hidden agenda.

A Few Steps Back, a Few Leaps Forward

Passive/aggressive behavior can be as mild as leaving our shoes lying around the house when we know it irritates our spouses, or as devastating as not allowing our children to have contact with their grandparents. Either way, it's a form of control that has its roots in serious problems.

In the last three chapters, we've discussed how control plays itself out in the home. Until we have a clear understanding of what *causes* us to control, however, we are lame to do anything about it. So in the next few chapters, we're going to learn what beats in the hearts of coercive personalities. These are the fragile flaws that turn well-meaning people into control brokers. For most of us, understanding the cause is going to be our best step toward a cure—our first step toward freedom.

Part Three

CHAPTER 7

Toxic Fear

ear is like a loaded gun. It's real handy if someone's trying to kill you, but dangerous if it's just lying around. Some people avoid fear at all cost, while others invest heavily in the sheer terror of it. Whether they're bungee jumping off a bridge, the stock market, or the marital altar, fear either fuels them, schools them, or fools them. And you can't predict how they'll respond. One person's motivation is another's paralysis—all because of this intangible force that haunts our souls and stalks us through our daily grind.

Fear Is a Four-Letter Word

God doesn't let us dance through life without, somewhere along the line, letting us do the mambo with fear. It's as much a part of our daily checklist as joy, confusion, exhilaration, or contentment. Some people understand fear better than others. We call them "courageous" people. They know that fear is the mettle within courage. They embrace it—making it their friend—so that it motivates them to do the right things at the right time, regardless of the cost.[1]

Fear is one of the greatest gifts God has placed in the arsenal of human emotions. Fear of financial disaster kicks us out of bed in the morning and pushes us into the rat race. Fear keeps us from getting into situations that are stacked against us. At the same time, fear gives us strength to prevail against those situations when they can't be avoided. Fear seizes us by the throat when the "mother of all temptations"—the kind that wrecks our marriages, our kids, and our reputations all at the same time—comes our way. If it were possible to calculate, we'd probably find that more families have been saved from moral ruin by raw fear than by some overwhelming devotion to a moral code.

That's the good news. Here's the bad news: Fear is a four-letter word. It can destroy the things you work for, defame the God you live for, and defraud the people for whom you'd be willing to die. Letting fear rule your family is not one of the seven deadly sins, but it ought to be.

We can further define the word *fear* by adding the adjective "toxic." *Toxic fear* is what you get when you let an unfortunate event (or series of unfortunate events) rule your life. It's the product of a long line of sleepless nights or of a lifetime of looking over your shoulder. Toxic fear may have its epicenter in an auto accident, a divorce, a financial betrayal, a house fire, or the death of a loved one. Those are the bigger-than-life events that make or break you. Somewhere deep in your unconscious, such happenings drop a seed of fear. How you respond in the aftermath determines whether the seed dies or takes root.

People seldom realize how much the fear resulting from these events can manipulate their lives and ultimately motivate them to control people around them. But it can, and it does. Toxic fear is one of the five major reasons people develop high-control patterns in their lives. It may take years for the effects of fear to demonstrate themselves in controlling patterns, and when they do, the controlling person is usually oblivious to the source.

A case in point was Craig. He didn't realize, until it was too late, that fear had turned him into a control freak. Let me explain.

As a boy, Craig watched three things happen that turned him into an overcontrolling husband. First, he watched his mother sneak behind his father's back to pursue other men. In the beginning, he tried to trivialize her illicit relationships as innocent friendships. After all, some of the guys played softball with his father. But all that changed when he came home from school one midday to discover his mother in her nightgown and one of his father's "friends" in her arms.

She was obviously shaken by his sudden appearance and fled to her bedroom, slamming the door behind her. That's when the guy grabbed Craig by the front of his shirt, threw him against the refrigerator door, and threatened him with extinction if he breathed a word to anybody about what he'd seen.

The second thing that happened was the explosion between his mother and father when his dad finally learned what everyone else in town already knew. He handled his heartbreak with violence, but not toward Craig's mother. Rather, the violence was directed at Craig. His dad's misdirected anger was too complicated for Craig to process. He was too young, his emotional system too undeveloped, for him to figure out why he became the whipping boy for his mother's sins. He couldn't figure out the ambivalence that wrestled within his father's heart—he still loved his wife yet wanted to punish her. Rather than strike her, he struck the one person he knew she loved more than herself—Craig.

The third part of the nightmare was the inevitable divorce and the bitter custody battle that accompanied it. Craig could have quickly determined the outcome by telling the judge about the physical beatings he'd taken from his dad. But he kept it all inside, hoping it was just a temporary glitch in his father's behavior. Craig became the rope in a tug-of-war between the two people he loved the most. And in the process, they wrung out on the courtroom floor whatever confidence he had in himself.

The fear that gripped his heart during the clandestine affairs, the violence from his father, and the aftermath of the custody battle drove Craig to take control of any and every detail that he felt could threaten his security. He'd learned what happens when your love is left uncontrolled and at the mercy of someone else, so he felt driven to make sure that nothing and nobody could ever threaten his heart again.

Years after his unfortunate childhood experiences, Craig married Kelly. From the outset, fear took control of the marriage. Unconsciously but deliberately, Craig found himself compelled to take control of the most minor nuances of his wife's life. He didn't pick out Kelly's wardrobe, but he made *suggestions* she felt required to follow. He determined the length and style of her hair. In both clothing and hair, one word could be used to describe his taste—*modest*. Kelly went from a stylish, attractive girl before marriage to a frumpy, plain Jane after.

Craig didn't have any outside interests, and he threw a wet blanket over any suggestion that they develop close friendships. When a clipboard was passed in Sunday school class to sign up for the next social, Kelly would fill in their names, and Craig would cross them out.

About two years into their marriage, Craig came up with an idea he thought Kelly would love. He had always used an elaborate calendar organizer to track his daily schedule. Appointments, phone calls, checklists, and chores were all written there. And on one of their weekly dates, he gave Kelly her own pocket organizer. He had wrapped it like a birthday gift and made a big speech about how much he appreciated the work she did both inside and outside the house. His gift, he told her, would enable her to track her time better and stuff more productive hours into her day.

Kelly wasn't the checklist-and-paper-clip type. She had no trouble with hard work, and she was thorough in all she did. But her personality didn't align with the meticulous detail that Craig's organizer required. Even more difficult to appreciate was the verbal commitment that was to go with his gift. She was to agree to keep a careful account of each moment of her day, and then, on Thursday evening, they would exchange notebooks and look over each other's past week.

She said it wasn't necessary for him to give account of his week to her. "You're a big boy, Honey, and a responsible one. I'm confident you're making the most of your time."

He rebuffed her and made it clear that he felt keeping track would be good for *both* of them. And so the scrutiny began. Every Thursday, he would probe the who, what, where, why, how, and when of her past week. Instead of its being a time of review, focus, and goal setting, the whole evening developed into an extended cross-examination. She found herself having to defend the times she put down for different tasks she did. He'd argue about the distance to the dry cleaners or the library and question the length of time it took her to go there. Kelly also found herself having to defend every conversation she had on the phone or with people she encountered throughout her day.

After a few months of this, she appealed to their pastor. He convinced Craig to back off on the Thursday-night reviews and suggested some serious marriage counseling for them. Craig reacted to the suggestion as though it were a personal affront. Kelly was glad when he finally let up on the inquisition, even though he was unwilling to go for counseling. But all of Craig's promises to lighten up were temporary. Too soon, she again found herself under Craig's microscope.

Their marriage lasted six years before everything Craig feared and tried to control against came to pass. Kelly traded prison at home for guilt in the arms of another man. Craig lost everything he longed for because he imprisoned love that was meant to bask in the sunlight of grace.

As noted earlier, fear is one of God's many gifts. The right kind of fear protects us, warns us, and helps us learn valuable lessons. But Craig was mastered not by good fear, but by toxic fear. The nightmares he lived through as a child pushed him to take control of situations in ways that exceeded his God-given responsibility. He thought that making Kelly frumpy would keep guys away. He thought that avoiding social settings would minimize the chance some other man might turn her head away from him. His fear made him so desperate that he actually believed coercing Kelly to account for her use of time could keep her heart from straying. His story paints a vivid picture of what toxic fear does to us if it is not placed at the foot of the cross.

Had Craig learned to utilize God's gift of forgiveness toward his parents, as well as appropriating God's power to love and trust his wife, he would have known he could not maintain fidelity through emotional bondage. When he failed to process the fears from his childhood properly, they turned toxic and ultimately poisoned the love between Kelly and himself. He was an extreme example of what happens when fear moves from being an ally to an enemy. It's a phenomenon that has been corrupting relationships since the beginning of time.

Life is a series of question marks. Lots of things happen that are out of our realm or capability to control. That's when we need a big God to lean on. But when people instead let fear get the best of them, high control is often the method they appropriate to cope.

That's what Adam and Eve turned to when they first sinned. Fear drove them to think they could manipulate themselves out of their dilemma. Fear came shortly after they trifled with the forbidden fruit. The first thing they realized, once they had sinned, was that they were naked. Right away, they wanted to do something to solve their moral crisis short of coming clean with God and asking for forgiveness. That's how they ended up sewing a bunch of leaves together and wrapping them around themselves to cover their nakedness. Let's pick up the drama in Genesis 3:7-10:

> Then the eyes of both of them were opened, and they knew that they were naked; and they sewed fig leaves together and made themselves loin coverings. And they heard the sound of the Lord God walking in the garden in the cool of the day, and the man and his wife hid themselves from the presence of the Lord God among the trees of the garden. Then the Lord God called to the man, and said to him, "Where are you?" And he said, "I heard the sound of Thee in the garden, and I was afraid because I was naked; so I hid myself."

"I was afraid ... so I hid." We could paraphrase this, "I was afraid, so I took matters into my own hands—I controlled." Adam, like Craig, thought he could manipulate outcomes by controlling those he had no right to control. Adam wasn't authorized to control God or Eve, but fear compelled him to try. History is the footnote of his attempt.

Holding the Things We Love in an Open Palm

My youngest daughter, Shiloh, was taking a walk with me one hot summer afternoon. We were walking through a pasture near the cabin where we were staying on vacation in East Texas. The edge of the pasture was lined with wildflowers. Like most little girls, Shiloh wanted to pick a

74

bouquet to take back to her mother. I walked beside her as she hopped from one group of flowers to the next, carefully arranging a nice assortment in her hand. When she thought it was perfect, we made our way up the path, through the woods, toward the cabin.

I noticed that Shiloh was being extremely careful with the flowers, perhaps a little too careful. We stopped to rest a minute, and I suggested she not squeeze the flowers so tightly. "Flowers are very delicate, Shiloh," I said. "If you grip too tightly, they wilt and fade from the pressure."

"But Daddy," she answered, "if I don't hold them real tight, I'm afraid I'll lose one."

Some lessons are best learned the hard way. There would be more walks to the pasture and a fresh crop of wildflowers to pick. We detoured from the direct route to our cabin in order to stop by a soft drink machine. The choke hold she maintained on the flowers during our 20-minute detour zapped them of their beauty. By the time we got to the cabin, not even fresh water could revive them. They were little more than a handful of weeds.

Shiloh's the "Mother Teresa" of our family. She is so filled with compassion and sympathy that when things don't work out the way she hoped, she is overwhelmed by grief. Her tears for the flowers gave me an opportunity to sit her on my lap and talk a bit about gentle love.

The people we love are just like those flowers—they wilt under unnecessary pressure. When fear compels us to control, we need to step back and see where that action will ultimately lead. Fear makes us think our problems can be solved if we just hold on a little tighter to the things and people we love the most. In the end, that kind of control destroys the confidence and trust that make relationships strong. God has provided a way to keep fear from getting the best of us. But it requires that we put our confidence in Him and His ability to work in and through the people and circumstances in our lives.

Hope for Those Who Suffer Toxic Fear

Craig and the others who control from a platform of fear need to take God at His word. The Bible says a lot of encouraging things to those who fear to a fault. God understands our propensity for trying to take control of things that aren't our responsibility. He knows how much better we would fare if we simply placed our confidence in Him. Listen, please, to what He has to say:

The Lord is my light and my salvation; whom shall I fear? The Lord is the defense of my life; whom shall I dread?

Psalm 27:1

For you have not received a spirit of slavery leading to fear again, but you have received a spirit of adoption as sons.

Romans 8:15

For God has not given us a spirit of timidity [fear], but of power and love and discipline.

2 Timothy 1:7

There is no fear in love; but perfect love casts out fear, because fear involves punishment, and the one who fears is not perfected in love.

1 John 4:18

Toxic fear. When the things that haunt us drive us to overstep our bounds and begin to control the people we love, we have tainted our commitment to them. But we'll see later that it doesn't have to be this way.

Fear is one of five forces within that can turn toxic enough to make us high controllers. In the next chapter, we're going to see another problem that keeps its pilot light burning in every human heart.

CHAPTER 8

Toxic Rage

Squirrel season, Watauga County, North Carolina, October 1962. Dawn. The explosion of the 16-gauge shotgun broke the silence. The muted thud of a man's body falling into the leaves was followed by the distinct shout of his comrade. Then the long, pregnant silence gradually gave way to the deep-from-the-chest wails of anguished crying.

It was such a freak accident. When you read these stories in the paper, you just shake your head and say, "What a shame!" What we seldom see is how these accidents affect the lives of the individuals involved. But with this one, I did. Up close. Personal. It was, indeed, a shame!

My path crossed Peter's when we were both in our early twenties. At that time, it had been ten years since his father was killed while squirrel hunting. Ten years since Peter's confidence had been extinguished by a shotgun blast.

His father had been hunting with a friend when they came to a barbed-wire fence. The rules of gun safety dictate that, in this situation, hunters should unload their guns and place them through the fence, on the ground on the other side, before slipping their bodies between the wires. But for some reason, these men had placed their loaded guns through the fence on the other side and leaned the barrels against the middle wire. The jostling of the wire as Peter's father passed through caused his friend's gun to fall against the fence post and discharge. Peter's dad died about a minute after he fell to the ground.

Peter was 11 years old when this tragedy left him fatherless. I don't suppose there's an ideal time for a boy to have to bury his dad, but there are some years when a father's death can have a greater negative effect than at others. Peter was standing at the threshold of puberty—the starting block of adulthood. He was coming to those critical years when the wisdom and insight of a father plays a key role in the completion of a boy's value system. But Peter had to go it alone.

Since he was his parents' only child, the death had a radical impact on the dynamic between him and his mother. With his confidence already wounded, he found his grieving complicated by the enormous expectations his mother placed on him. She turned to him to shoulder many of the responsibilities his father had carried. Her actions were deliberate. She had become convinced, through the advice of friends, that giving Peter a more mature role would help him process his loss better. She was wrong.

Perhaps Peter would have been okay if he'd been able to talk out the confusing feelings in his heart with someone close to him. Instead, he suffered in silence.

Somewhere between the funeral and the time I met Peter, his suffering had turned into seething rage. He was 21 years old and had a boulder-sized chip on his shoulder. But now, his rage compelled him to try to control everything and everyone he cared about.

I watched him control his mother, who had become almost totally dependent on him. He controlled the family finances to such an extent that she literally worked for the estate (a combination of what his father had accumulated and insurance settlements). A financial advisor had worked with his mother until Peter was 18, but then Peter convinced her to let him make the investment choices. Fortunately for them, he knew enough to protect their net worth. The result of the arrangement, however, was that he paid his mother a stipend from the trust and made her put in requests for any purchases above her allotment.

Peter was also the reason she hadn't remarried. She had been interested in two different men during the ten-year span since her husband's death, but he had reacted negatively to both. He made life miserable for his mother's romantic interests, and in the process he convinced her that bringing a stepfather into the picture would not work. He had idealized his father in death, making him greater than he ever was in life. Peter was committed to the idea that the only person who could fill his father's position in the home was himself.

When Peter went to college, he tried to expand his sphere of control. Most of the guys he hung around with simply ignored his attempts. His girlfriend had a tougher go of it. She genuinely cared for him, but she was smothered by his dominating presence in her life. He manipulated details of her life that most outsiders felt were none of his business. I remember seeing him sitting beside her as she talked with her academic advisor. He wasn't just sitting, however; he was arguing with the advisor over the courses she should be taking. He wanted her to change majors. His wishes were not only in opposition to hers, but also to her advisor's and her parents', who were paying for her education. Her parents prevailed upon her to continue with her academic strategy, but it was the only battle they won over Peter. He ultimately married the girl, and he hasn't lost a battle since.

Fire Burn and Caldron Bubble

Peter controlled because he was angry. A rage seethed just below the surface of every decision he made on behalf of the people around him. He was a screaming tea kettle that no one seemed able to hear. He was filled with toxic rage.

How do I know? He told me so.

At that time in my life, I wasn't sophisticated enough intellectually or emotionally to ask the right questions or draw the proper conclusions for his life. But I didn't need to be. His behavior was blatant enough, and his comments about his life were obvious enough, to put all the pieces of the puzzle together. Obviously, his kind of problems are extremely complicated, and I'm not suggesting some simple analysis of his nightmare. But the diagnosis is obvious.

Peter was angry at his father for being careless. Although he felt the normal sorrow, pity, and loss that should accompany this kind of tragedy, when the surface emotions played themselves out, the underlying emotion that survived was anger.

"How could he be such a jerk?" He broke the silence with that question as we walked back to the dorm from the administration building one evening.

"How could *who* be such a jerk?" I asked.

Then he told me about the accident that took his father's life. I tried to assure him his father never meant to be careless or irresponsible. If we could change one or two details of any tragedy, we could alter its outcome. But wishing circumstances had been different wasn't going to change anything for Peter. We talked until the wee hours of the morning about his mixed feelings of deep love for and, at the same time, incredible disappointment in his father.

Peter was also angry at his mother—angry that she had refused to let him go hunting with his father that tragic morning. That had been the original plan, but Peter had come down with a cold, and his mother had insisted he stay home. He felt that if he had been there, he could have prevented the accident.

He was also angry at God. He felt God had robbed him of his father. This showed itself in overt antagonism to spiritual issues, and also in frequent attempts to throw a verbal wet blanket over other people's confidence in the Lord.

When Anger Turns Inward

Anger is another of the greatest gifts God has given our emotional system. It's one of the things that puts courage into our convictions, resolve into our aspirations, and tenacity into our actions. It is a holy loathing that keeps us from surrendering strongholds to the moral enemies of the soul. You can't love without anger. But you can be angry without love.

That's when anger turns toxic. Like an emotional cancer, toxic anger eats away at our courage, our resolve, and our tenacity. It leaves our love anemic. But it doesn't go naked. That would be intolerable to our system. Instead, toxic rage clothes itself in control.

Emotions, as we all know, are extremely sophisticated. They operate like independent organisms that are in a constant state of adjustment to the events affecting them. When we experience traumatic emotional pain, anger is one of the legitimate ways we react. But somewhere along the line, our anger needs to be resolved. If it isn't, it turns to rage and sets off a series of reactions that leave us at the mercy of that rage. Overcontrol is one of the standard ways we cope with open-ended, unresolved anger.

The laundry list of "events" that can turn rage into high control is endless. It includes, among many other things:

- perfectionist parents
- the divorce of our parents
- our own divorce
- cruel treatment from an ex-spouse
- a crippling illness
- a terminal illness
- inequities at work
- killer gossip
- being fat in a thin world
- being average in a smart-person's world
- being single in a partnered world
- being young in an adult world
- being old in a young world
- being inadequate in a world that shows no grace
- abuse of any kind

Anger turns toxic when people refuse to show understanding or mercy. We would not expect average people to be capable of showing mercy or understanding at the initial event that causes their anger. But somewhere along the line, we need to weigh our disappointments on accurate scales and deal with them.

Peter, like so many people whose hearts are shattered, didn't have the maturity at the time the accident happened, and he wasn't offered the counseling that could have helped him process his pain properly. Because of this unfortunate set of circumstances, he relived his father's loss every time he exercised coercion against another. He couldn't free his heart to enjoy his father's memory or to build and grow from his father's 11-year influence.

Somewhere back there, Peter's anger had slipped over a line and turned into toxic rage. And since no one could hear the screams from his heart, he turned to manipulation on the outside.

What's interesting about Peter is how his rage ultimately worked out. He became the unwitting head of his household with a vengeance. Sometimes rage acts itself out in extremely noble but nonetheless controlling ways. Rage can push a person to perfectionism, to inordinate servanthood, or to deceptive agreeableness. Sometimes the angry person uses overt generosity to keep another off balance. Whatever the means, anger does a number on families, and the angry controller is often the last to realize his control is fueled by deeply imbedded hostility.

I've been using the words *anger* and *rage* interchangeably, but technically they're two different degrees of pain. Anger, in and of itself, is a legitimate and helpful emotion. It's the normal emotional response to events or consequences that have induced intense displeasure. Although not without conditions, it has a positive use that is encouraged in the Bible.[1] Anger is a normal part of the emotional package of a healthy person. It might be utilized on a daily basis.

Anger has a built-in drawback, however. It's difficult to display without evoking a similar reaction from the people toward whom it is directed. That's the way it is for all the emotions. They're contagious. Happy people make those around them happy. Melancholy people can bring others down. And sympathetic people draw others to themselves because of their tenderness.

Happy, moody, or sympathetic is one thing; angry is something else. Anger begets anger. My updated paraphrase of Proverbs 15:1 is "A soft answer turns away wrath, but harsh words tick people off." Not only does anger have a negative effect on those upon whom it's poured, but it also wreaks havoc in the hearts of those who don't have a legitimate and regular outlet for expressing it.

Millions of people were raised in homes where they were not free to express disappointment, hurt, or frustration, especially toward their parents or God.

When anger is not properly processed, it turns to rage. Rage is anger out of control. It can easily border on violence and lead to abuse. *Abuse* can be defined as one person controlling another when he himself is out of control. Overstepping our boundaries stirs up intense frustration, anger, and even rage in another and thereby propagates the nightmare of toxic rage.

Fear Begets Anger

In the last chapter, we saw how fear can cause us to manipulate. But anger is often the logical result of fear that is improperly processed. The ghosts that haunted Peter's soul, for instance, would frighten any 11-year-old: The violent moment when the gun went off, the moment his mother told him his father was dead, the funeral home, the hearse, the graveyard, the whispers at school, the lack of a male voice cheering him on from the stands, the empty chair at the dinner table night after night. The helplessness felt in those moments calls for some type of coping mechanism. Since fear and anger are kissing cousins, it's only natural a person would turn his fear into control.

The most controlling woman I've ever known is on a New England church staff. Our paths have crossed many times. She lives on "high beam" and has successfully controlled the people in her inner circle without losing her job. How? I don't know. On a recent visit to her church, however, she told me and two of her associates a fact about her past that gave me a greater understanding of her overcontrol.

She's been raped. Twice.

It happened once while she was in college, and the second time about five years after she'd married. She said she lived in intense fear after the first incident. But after the second time, she simply got angry. The guy who committed this crime against her was brought to justice, but he walked out of the courtroom on technicalities. That's when she decided she was never going to let anything like that happen to her again. She acknowledged her anger has had a crippling effect on many of her vital relationships, and she is now committed to changing this dimension of her life.

No one blames a woman like that for being scared or angry. No one blames her for wanting to do what is within her power to make sure she's never raped again. But by her own confession, she feels her fear and rage have turned her into a woman she wishes she weren't.

Unresolved Anger and High Control

Why is it that anger, when left to fester in our hearts, leads us to become high controllers? Here are some of the reasons:

• Angry people are inherently suspicious.

They've been burned—by people or circumstances. They may even think God burned them. Their pain may have come in one resounding blow or in a series of jabs endured over a period of years. The effect is the same. Angry people are reluctant to trust. They're reluctant to put themselves in a position where they can be burned again.

• Angry people are mildly (if not in a major way) depressed.

Depression, in layman's terms, is when your emotions get the flu. Unless treated properly, anger-induced depression normally gets worse.

If you worked out on a stair-step machine for, say, eight hours (!), your body would get completely exhausted. For the next three or four days, you might have an agenda that required your body to take you different places or perform with skill, but it would say, "Tough! I'm not budging from this bed until I recover from all that exertion." In the same way, prolonged demands on our emotions call for pockets of rest—days when we don't make any major demands on them or expect them to be reliable.

Many people are depressed after they come home from a honeymoon, after the big victory, or after they've given birth. The emotions are simply saying, "I've had it. Give me a break for a few days so I can regroup and come back strong."

If people endure years of emotional diatribes and verbal ambushes within their homes, it only stands to reason that their spirits will take a nosedive. Without an outlet, depression is inevitable. "Depression results in those children who [for instance] were punished when they spoke up or showed anger. In this way they were conditioned to keep their angry feelings inside."[2]

Depression obviously keeps us in a discouraged mode, and discouraged people will control others in an effort to minimize their internal pain.

• Angry people have a fundamental drive to make things fair, but they

84

often lack the objectivity or power to do it without controlling people they shouldn't.

Life isn't fair. But when it's consistently unfair, people get desperate. When the inequities we suffer accumulate enough to make us want to even things up, overcontrol isn't far behind. Anger drives us to make things right, even if we have to be wrong in the process.

• Angry people are punitive.

Unresolved disappointments make people feel as though something is owed them. When they don't get what they inherently think they deserve (e.g., understanding, sympathy, freedom, or help), they feel justified in making life uncomfortable for others.

"I never got to have a car when I was 16 years old, so I don't see why you should." This kind of reasoning (or lack of it) falls from the lips of parents all the time. Whether or not a teenager should have a car of his own shouldn't be determined by a parent's disappointing childhood. The responsibility level of the teenager, the financial options of the parents, the geographic area in which they live, and the necessities of family members may rule out a personal car for a 16-year-old. Either way, the decision should be based on those kinds of reasons. When we instead make decrees that are clearly attached to wrongs we suffered, the people involved will feel emotionally abused.

• Angry people are tired.

It takes a lot of energy to maintain anger over a prolonged period. One has to file disappointments, log injustices, and store grudges within the soul. That's hard to do without ultimately expecting others to help carry the burden. Because of the energy required to keep the fire within an angry person's gut blazing, he or she aligns the lives of loved ones in a way that minimizes frustrations. An angry mother, for example, can make life around the living room unlivable. Hers is a restless heart longing for relief. But her unwillingness to relinquish her anger denies her heart that aid. This brings up the last observation about unresolved anger.

• Angry people are lazy.

Relinquishing anger takes a commitment of the heart that is, taxing to the soul. Obviously, people who relinquish their anger must surrender their right to get even. That takes guts. They have to make themselves emotionally vulnerable (maybe even to those they hold responsible for their pain—like God). The hurts they've already endured make that option appear unacceptable. They may have to forgive people who have never acknowledged the extent of the crimes they've perpetuated. That doesn't seem fair. And, most of all, angry people may have to look into their souls and acknowledge their own responsibility for the pain they've paid out over the years.

Eat Crow or Die

I'd like to summarize this chapter with the words of author Frederick Buechner. Buechner understands the long-term effect of toxic rage. He sees beyond the moment and factors in the truth. And with his weighted and wise words, he explains why unresolved anger, when all is said and done, simply costs too much. On page 2 of his winsome book *Wishful Thinking: A Theological ABC*, he puts it like this:

> Of the Seven Deadly Sins, anger is possibly the most fun. To lick your wounds, to smack your lips over grievances long past, to roll over your tongue the prospect of bitter confrontations still to come, to savor to the last toothsome morsel both the pain you are given and the pain you are giving back—in many ways it is a feast fit for a king. The chief drawback is that what you are wolfing down is yourself. The skeleton at the feast is you.[3]

When our anger drives us toward overcontrol, sometimes the people we love the most get caught in the grinder.

Proverbs 13:12 says, *"Hope deferred makes the heart sick."* A childhood without hope of relief from unpleasant experiences all but guarantees an adulthood of overcontrol. It's the only way some people feel they can be assured they won't fall into the same trap again. Unfortunately, it guarantees the opposite. Dr. Paul Gelinas says it this way: "In my years as a clinical psychologist working with young adults, I cannot recall a single case of neurosis or emotional disturbance that did not have anger as the main or intrinsic element in the disorder."[4]

Toxic rage! It turns nice people into controlaholics. Everybody suffers from the schemes and outbursts of those who have been unable or unwilling to close the loop on their rage.[5] Angry overcontrollers work against the best interests of everyone who matters in their lives, and, without help, they're usually destined to spend a good part of their lives isolated from the close, vulnerable type of love that makes relationships strong.

We've now discussed two poisons that drive people to control: fear and anger. In the next chapter, we'll see what happens when these two are mixed with the unspeakable. But one parting word about anger.

"For the anger of man does not achieve the righteousness of God"
James 1:20.

CHAPTER 9

Toxic Shame

Meet Harry. When I first stepped inside his family circle, I felt like a person with the key to a side door of the Oval Office. Harry was one of the most influential "movers and shakers" in our community. His kids held the top positions on the academic, social, and athletic ladders at school. They were the Kennedys of my neighborhood.

Because of my close friendship with his kids, I found myself on a first-name basis with Harry. In the process, I developed a whole new meaning to the expression "tough love." For the handful of us invited past the arches of his living room and into the kitchen to join the private conversations between family members, Harry presented one of the greatest challenges ever to our young psyches. Harry was a control czar. He gave me the best lesson, in a negative sense, in how to maintain a commitment to someone in spite of the treatment received.

I first met Harry when I was a teenager, and I've remained close to his family up to the present. Harry died some years back. While he lived, his control over his children was so strong that it lingers in behavioral patterns they still struggle with today. It's as though he pulls their strings from his grave.

Harry tried but failed to control me, too, which probably explains my longevity as a friend to him and his family. There was one primary reason his emotional muscles couldn't get the best of me—*he couldn't get me to fear him.* That's also the best explanation for the mutual respect we shared in the last few years of his life.

It's too bad Harry and his children never gained the closeness for which they longed. His vulnerability as a father was inhibited by the shroud he kept over his childhood. It wasn't until after he died—when he could no longer keep the curtain tightly drawn around his past—that the true depth of his pain could be felt. Had he been courageous enough to share it with his family from the beginning, I know he would have received the understanding required to make him the vulnerable and loving husband and father they needed. Unfortunately, he refused. Because of that, when his children stood beside his grave, for the most part they bid farewell to a stranger.

A Crying Shame

When Harry was a teenager, his parents found their relationship struggling for survival. It was the late 1930s. Work was scarce, and so was money. Harry's mother had social tastes that his father never seemed able to afford. They were both Russian immigrants. He came with the Old-World commitment to hard work. She came with a New-World commitment to the good life. Neither had any modeling or training to show them how to work through this kind of marital difference.

By and by, she went looking for superficial fulfillment in the arms of another man. When Harry's father discovered his wife's unfaithfulness, he couldn't deal with his broken heart and the humiliation that overwhelmed him. Rather than attack her or her lover, he turned his anger on himself. Disgusted with his own inadequacy and broken by his wife's abandonment, Harry's father went to an isolated location and hung himself. The day Harry's father took his life, he also took his son's life. For it was this event that began Harry's own war with the most debilitating of all emotions—shame.

When his mother saw what her betrayal had done, she snapped. She was disgusted with herself and overwhelmed with guilt. Her internal war got so bad that she had to be committed to a mental institution. This left Harry to finish high school as the kid whose father hung himself and whose mother was in the "nut house." The shame intensified.

Being the oldest child, Harry had to pick up a lot of the responsibility of providing for his siblings. And with the world gearing up for war, he felt not only the emotional instability of being in a family with no sense of cohesion, but also the instability of living in a world filled with nations itching to cut each others' throats.

After a while, his mother started to show improvement. The doctors thought a weekend outside the oppressive environment of the hospital might help rebuild her confidence. So she went to be with one of her friends. A wedding was going on that Saturday afternoon at a church just down the street from the friend's house. The friend left Harry's mother alone for a few minutes to go see the couple exchange vows. When the woman came back, she found Harry's mother in the basement. She had hung herself.

A double suicide is more than any person is designed to process. For Harry, the shame that overcame him when his mother also committed suicide killed what little hope he had left of ever being able to enjoy a normal life. In his small town, being the oldest son of parents who did "you know what" was tantamount to having to wear the scarlet letter.

After a while, however, Harry found love. But even though his wife knew his family history, he forbade her from breathing a word to anyone else. He wanted to deal with it by acting as if it had never happened. He made the choice to block out his youth. That choice locked him into the high-control life-style that stalked him the rest of his days.

Harry devoted the bulk of his professional life to trying to do good for other people. It was a cathartic attempt to gain closure on his shameful past. Unfortunately, he couldn't figure out how to bring his benevolence home long enough to touch his children with the love wandering around in his broken heart. His kindness was the antiseptic brand you give to strangers who will never know the real you.

When I got the phone call saying Harry had died, I prayed for those he left behind. I asked that somehow, God would give them the power to forgive him. Once his funeral was behind everyone, his wife broke the silence. In the process of filling in the missing pieces of the puzzle, I gained a new understanding of the tragedy that summed up his life. Unfortunately, the answers to the mystery came too late to enable the people who loved him the most to help him—and too late to stop the damage his shame brought upon those he left behind.

The Master Emotion

Shame is now called "the master emotion, the unseen regulator of our entire affective life."[1] It, among all the emotions, is the preeminent catalyst of emotional pain in our modern era. As we have observed, it can haunt a family for generations. Shame is often the "cause of the cause."

In the last two chapters, we discussed how some people are pulled into controlling patterns by events that resulted in either inordinate fear or unbridled rage. But shame is often the catalytic emotion that makes their fear and rage so compelling. Why? Because at the core of the controller's heart, his sense of utter shame blocks his ability to see himself as anything but fundamentally and absolutely flawed.

That's the crux of the problem. Shame, different from any other emotion, completely redefines the individual's view of his own self-worth. The kind of emotional pain attached to shame is so severe that few can resist the urge to manipulate others in an effort to protect themselves from further pain.

Embarrassment, Guilt, Shame—What's the Difference?

I remember one time when I pulled a "President Bush" in front of a group of men. It was at a marriage conference in which the men and women were separated for the session. I, of course, was addressing the men, and as I came to the lectern, I noticed a lady sitting in our midst. I made a few jokes about having spies from the other session; I said one man had sent his wife to take notes for him while he stayed in his room and watched the football game. Finally I spoke directly to the woman to continue the fun—only to discover *she* was a *he*.

I was a 1960s kid. I should have known better than to assume long hair equaled a woman! The men had a great laugh—at my expense and, unfortunately, at the expense of the man to whom I had drawn attention. I was embarrassed! I was angry at myself for being so foolish.

What made matters worse was that about a year later, during a similar session in a marriage conference, I did *the exact same thing again!* I can assure you that in future men's-only sessions, even if I look out and see what I believe is a woman, my lips will be sealed.

You've experienced embarrassing moments like that before. And although we feel as if we want to die, those embarrassments are not terminal. For the most part, they get absorbed somewhere in our coping systems, and we move on. Normally we look back on them with a laugh and a nod for the lessons learned.

There's a another feeling that goes into operation early in our lives. As a child, I experienced this emotion when I found myself practicing inappropriate behavior. Something inside me flagged my emotions to tell me my behavior was wrong. The emotion was guilt.

Our consciences tell us, through guilt, when our actions are not meeting God's standard. Our guilty response to wrongdoing helps us maintain strong character, discretion, modesty, and respect for the standards and rights of other people. Guilt also causes a sorrow that leads to repentance, to a turning away from the wrongdoing toward right living. It warns of consequences, tugs at our hearts when we need to take responsibility for actions, accuses, and motivates us to make restitution. Guilt serves the human heart in ways designed to protect it.

There are two kinds of guilt—that imposed from the outside and that which is intrinsic, which comes from within. The guilt imposed from the outside is not good and can turn toxic when it moves over a line and behaves irrationally—when it's instilled in our hearts as children in such a way that we end up feeling responsible for things we never did. It's usually the result of someone's attempt to manipulate us, imposed in an effort to get us to do something the other person wants. It is closely tied to statements such as "You never call home. You don't love me." or "You're spending Christmas with them again. When do we get our turn?"

But productive, healthy, good guilt comes from within and is the result of a tender conscience and an openness to God and others. It's a subconscious reaction within our emotions that tells us to modify our behavior. We need to welcome good guilt as a friend, for it leads us away from sin and toward more prudent behavior. God meant it for our well-being.

It's important that we determine which kind of guilt we're feeling. If it's coming from the outside as an attempt to control us, we need to reject it. That kind of guilt destroys our self-esteem and turns us into people-pleasers who are always looking over our shoulders to avoid another confrontation.

If we're experiencing good guilt, however, we need to take appropriate action to correct the behavior producing it. It's not always easy to do, but there's good news. God sent His Son, Jesus Christ, to take away our guilt by removing the causes and giving us total forgiveness for what we've done.

Sometimes we confuse embarrassment and guilt with shame, probably because they produce the same kind of confused, uncomfortable feelings as shame. But shame, as the term is being used today, has a much deeper, more sinister meaning.

Life-style Shame: Outside In

A sad thing happened on our way to the twenty-first century. Shame took on an evil and sinister face, an ugliness and shabbiness that moved it to suppressed levels of the unspeakable and unacknowledged.

Actually, we've always had this brand of shame. But with the crumbling of the moral foundations within American families, we've seen this different face of shame raising its intimidating head in more homes than ever before. This kind of shame is the direct result of the increase in alcoholism, physical abuse, sexual abuse, absentee parents, and events such as the suicide of Harry's parents. Our homes are filled with parents shamed in their childhood and covering it now in their adult relationships. We have children who are being used and abused and told not to give away "our little secret," causing confusion and emotional pain that can last a lifetime.

These events have left our generation unsure about who we are. "Today, many psychologists believe that shame may be the core emotion from which all other negative ones receive their energy."²

This is what I call "life-style" or "destructive" shame. It serves no positive purpose in an individual's life. It debilitates a person, blocking the ability to give and receive love freely. That's because *it's imposed from the outside in*. It's foisted upon us by people who do not have our best interests at heart.

Shame literally means "to cover." It's the knee-jerk reaction to being too exposed or too vulnerable to other people. Shame is usually triggered by something that is done *to* us. This type of shame causes us to react differently to the events of life than does guilt. Guilt says we have done something wrong. Shame says that it is *we* who are wrong, that we're not good enough. Life-style shame is vulnerability out of control. It changes the way we evaluate our behavior, causing us to be unable to separate what we've done from who we are.

"Shame is less about morality than conformity, acceptability, or character. To be ashamed is to *expect* rejection, not so much because of what one has done as because of what one is. . . . Pathological [toxic] shame is an irrational sense of defectiveness, a feeling not of having crossed to the wrong side of the boundary but of having been born there," says Robert Karen.³

If people are guilty, they can simply fess up and pay up to eliminate their pain. Shame doesn't work that way. It's not so much a statement about what you did as much as it is about who you are—that you're foolish, stupid, or ugly—and that you shouldn't have been that way in the first place.

The Roots of Shame

For most people, shame has its roots in the past, usually in childhood. Because it is such a powerful emotion, some parents use it as a means of punishment. They know how effective shame can be in bringing a child into compliance with their wishes. A parent might wave a finger before the eyes of a child, yelling, "You should be ashamed of yourself!" The parent might temporarily abandon the child, turning from and shunning him at the very moment he needs to feel that although his actions were wrong, he is still accepted. The silence and rejection of his parents make the child feel shamed.

Ostracism, rebuke, a contemptuous tone of voice, threats, teasing, or other forms of emotional ventilation from a parent can also produce shame in the child, wounding his inner self, giving him a feeling of being fundamentally flawed—deformed at the core of his being.

We can't speak about the roots of shame without mentioning the effect abuse has on the human heart. Sexual, physical, and emotional abuse degrade a child at the deepest level. Abuse always results in shame. The betrayal involved in these kinds of abuse nearly always results in creating a high controller. So desperate are abused people to keep from ever being betrayed again, they will control every situation in order to avoid repeating the past.

Honest parents have to take a look at their own childhoods. They can't discount the role shame might be playing in their own lives. Their lives may be a collection of unmet needs, bitter disappointments, and unresolved anger. This could hamper them in their desire to accept their own children for who and what they really are. Their expectations may be light years from the children's capabilities. They want their kids to be smarter, prettier, friendlier, more charming, more affectionate, more aggressive, more articulate, more compliant—all because the parents are haunted by shame and want their children to fill the voids in their own lives.

These parents may fall short of transferring high value by withholding respect or tolerance for their children's uniqueness. This environment of abuse, periodic rejection, or insensitivity steadily chips away at children's views of themselves. It doesn't take long for kids to look in the mirror and only feel shame for what they see.

I knew a man in ministry who carried intense shame into his calling. He tried to use his ministry to salve some of the wounds from his past (an unfortunate decision). His wife gave him three fine sons. But he only saw them as obstacles to his "work for God." Not only did they represent a distraction to him, but when their behavior fell short of the ridiculously high standards he expected of them, even though they were mere children, he shamed them. And to keep them from slipping up, he dictated more rules with each mistake they made.

I met those boys. They felt so valueless that every time I was around them, I wanted to hug them and say how proud I was of them. I wanted to do anything I could to counter the negative input they received from their father. How do you think he perceived my actions? You guessed it—he felt even more ashamed. Shame had such a hold on him that there was little good anyone could do for him without his reacting. He felt so evil about himself that he couldn't receive love or grace from the people who were willing to help him.

The good news is that this man isolated his problem. Once he saw how shame played such a great role in his own life, he was able to take steps toward freeing his boys from the oppression they had endured.

He knows he's already passed on some shame to them. It's part of the plague that goes with it. Shame is transferable. Like a life-sucking lichen on a family tree, it can encompass centuries of limbs. "Nothing, apparently, defends against the internal ravages of shame more than the security gained from parental love, especially the sort of sensitive love that sees and appreciates the child for what he or she is and is respectful of the child's feelings, differences, and peculiarities. Nothing seems to make shame cut more deeply than the lack of that love."[4]

Cheap Praise

One of the ways we can set up our children to experience shame is to offer them what I call "cheap praise." (Praise that comes easily from our lips, but costs us nothing when it comes to our time, energy, and focus.) Can parents praise their children too much? Probably not. Can parents praise children in a wrong way? Yes, definitely, and it sets them up to feel shame.

Praise transfers best in an atmosphere that takes into account children's strengths and limitations. It factors in their likes and dislikes. And it hits the mark best when it is delivered with a commitment attached. That commitment is to building their moral character. It's the best way to insure that *what* we praise our children for is *what ultimately defines them.*

Our kids are great, but they will only remain great if we back our praise with a plan for helping them maximize their potential. It's easier to give praise than it is to give time. But praise without a plan to build their internal assets yields a sense of void rather than value. It's like building a beautiful home without a foundation and strong infrastructure. It may get to be the subject of a pictorial essay in *House Beautiful,* but you don't want to see what's left of it the first time it has to endure serious weather.

Unfortunately, some parents control with praise. When this happens, ultimately the children focus on their inadequacies as they consistently fall short of the phantom people their parents made them out to be. "Cheap praise", such as I've been describing, creates within children an over-whelming sense of being internally flawed.

The No-Talk Rule

As mentioned before, shame can be passed down from one generation to another. It can be a sad kind of family inheritance, as Harry so painfully found out. Families institute the no-talk rule to try to hide the deep, dark secrets that haunt them. This rule forces all the people in the family to become manipulative. "Stories of inherited shame uncover poverty resulting from bankruptcies, suicides, childhood deaths and accidents where the parents feel they were to blame (or were being punished), or secrets surrounding pregnancies, births, and adoptions."[5]

Family secrets can make overcontrollers out of every person in the family circle. A wife might be overly controlling because of the shame she feels for being pregnant when she got married. A husband might develop addictive patterns because he knows his wife's control is her way of saying, "You messed up my life once, but I'll be darned if I'll let you do it again." She ends up parenting him and compounds his sense of inadequacy as a partner, provider, and parent. His addiction becomes his way of dealing with his own shame. Out of sheer survival instincts, the children become controllers, too.

Shame's Bottom Line: Control

Shame plays out its hand in a lot of destructive ways: perfectionism, judgmental attitudes, addictions, compulsions, silence—you name it, shame uses it. Shame is not only the cause of a lot of people's controlling tendencies, but it's also the reason some people attach to (and at times seek out) controlling people to run their lives. They were taught they were inferior, bumbling incompetents or milquetoast pushovers. These painful attitudes toward themselves make them feel unworthy to have authority over the various dimensions of their lives.

Most often, shamed people take hold of as many of the variables as they can to protect themselves from further humiliation. They do this out of desperation. They control because they don't know any other way out of the nightmare. They experience, "Humiliation so painful, embarrassment so deep, and a sense of being so completely diminished that one feels he or she will disappear into a pile of ashes."[6]

Shame has a way of reproducing itself. That's why it is essential that we deal honestly and sensitively with ourselves as well as those around us who might be caught in a control trap. We must stop passing shame from generation to generation.

God's Plan: Freedom from Shame

It was not part of God's original plan for His children to be oppressed by so much shame. When we visit the first couple shortly after God created them, we find an enlightening statement about the way they were designed to view themselves. *"And the man and his wife were both naked and were not ashamed"* (Genesis 2:25).

There was no need to cover their vulnerability. Their bodies were as bare as their souls, and it didn't bother them. That's because of the fellowship they enjoyed with their Creator. It freed them to be themselves and to accept each other for who they were and how God had made them.

Then sin came along, and as mentioned in an earlier chapter, the first thing they realized was that they were naked, vulnerable, and too exposed to the other. So they immediately moved to high control to try to hide their shame. They hid their nakedness from each other by making clothes of leaves, and they hid from God by taking refuge in the forest.[7]

God's immediate solution to their sin was to kill an animal and use it to cover them. It was the first blood sacrifice for shame, but it wasn't the last. God realized the depth of mankind's shame and the desperate position it put us in. That's why He made the ultimate sacrifice. He sent His Son to take away our guilt, to bear our hurt, and to lift it from our shoulders once and for all.

"He made Him who knew no sin to be sin on our behalf, that we might become the righteousness of God in Him" (2 Corinthians 5:21).

Jesus went to the cross to take away humanity's shame. He had to become humiliation and shame just to do it. He hung naked before the crowd. He hung defeated before the soldiers. He hung alone outside the gates of Jerusalem. But He felt that we were worth the cost, regardless of whether we agreed with His evaluation of us. Scripture puts it this way:

"Fixing our eyes on Jesus, the author and perfecter of faith, who for the joy set before Him endured the cross, despising the shame, and has sat down at the right hand of the throne of God" (Hebrews 12:2).

God wants to relieve relationships of the oppression that always accompanies high control. He wants to do it by treating the source of the problem. Toxic shame drives people to control or be controlled. But for those who turn to Him, there is a sweet release.

Two weeks before Harry died, he found that release. Both my wife, Darcy, and I had stayed close to him throughout our adult years. She was by his side the night he reached out to the Lord. In one fell swoop of grace, God lifted from his heart the shame that had plagued him all his life and set him free.

God wants to set families free from the compulsion to control. He wants to eliminate one of the most oppressing causes of it—shame. And for those who seek, there is much to find. For those who ask, there is much to gain.

The apostle Peter found this out. Jesus warned that public opinion was going to turn against Him. Peter told Jesus that even if everyone else turned against Him, he never would. Jesus let him know that before the rooster crowed the next morning, Peter would deny he even knew Jesus—three times. When Jesus most needed him, Peter let Him down. After he three times denied any connection to Jesus, sure enough, the rooster crowed. Peter had failed, and he ran on his "feet of clay" to a dark corner of town, where he wept bitterly.

But that isn't the end of the story. After Jesus' resurrection, He and Peter hadf a sensitive discussion during a stroll down an isolated beach. In the process, Jesus lifted Peter's head. He put sparkle back in his eyes and excitement back in his step. He forgave Peter and showed him a new and better way to live.

Years later, after establishing the church in Jerusalem and shortly before he courageously died a martyr's death, Peter took parchment and quill in hand and penned these words about the power Jesus has over shame:

"Therefore it is also contained in the Scripture, 'Behold, I lay in Zion a chief cornerstone, elect, precious, and he who believes on Him will by no means be put to shame'"(1 Peter 2:6, NKJV).

It's a promise that can set the shamed heart free. And it's a promise that can lift the scourge of shame off a family. . . . forever.

CHAPTER 10

Toxic Bondage

o you remember playing the childhood game "What's Wrong With This Picture?" A photo or drawing would be handed to you containing some inherent flaw. You were supposed to deduce, after studying it a while, what was either missing, added, or marred that made the point of the picture illogical. As I recall, the younger I was, the more obvious was the defect in the picture.

This game continues on into adult life, but the flaws in the pictures we stare at are far more subtle and camouflaged. We might stare at the pictures of our relationships for years and not realize they're cluttered with pain. That's what I felt in my acquaintance with Aaron.

On the front side of our contact with each other, it didn't occur to me that something might be muddled at the core of his life. I thought his struggles were probably no more or less than most human beings have when coping with their inadequacies and inner bents. Aaron had respect as a businessman, amateur athlete, and advisor. When it came to friendship, he was the kind of person who always made you feel good because you knew him.

He fell in love with Susan, one of the darlings of his church. This girl had such a pristine track record with God that any parent would have loved to claim her as a daughter. If it were your job to choose the participants in the Christmas pageant, you'd figure that giving her the part of Mary was type casting. Their courtship went through the normal struggles and adjustments until they came to the mutual conclusion that they were meant for each other. About the only thing that really seemed out of the ordinary was Aaron's overwhelming ambivalence about taking the final plunge into matrimony. It's normal for a certain amount of uncertainty to plague a courtship, but Aaron's was way beyond the norm.

As an outsider looking in, I thought the decision to marry Susan was a "no brainer." Most guys would jump at the chance of having her for a wife. Had I known then what I know now, Aaron's ambivalence would have made perfect sense.

Ultimately, the wedding took place. It was followed by six years of emotional bliss, financial success, and the logging of great memories. Aaron had me buffaloed for quite a while. But then my "eye for the distortion" started noticing a symptom of a deeper problem. Something about him seemed out of sync. At the time, I didn't feel I knew either of them well enough to pry, nor had I earned the right, but I was high enough on their friendship list to start feeling a few concerns. My "What's wrong with this picture?" mind-set kept eating away at me.

Though I didn't want to judge him unfairly, it dawned on me one day that Aaron paid an exorbitant amount of attention to the image he conveyed to people. This is fairly normal when one is a teenager, and most of us continue to be concerned about the way we're perceived even as adults. But there's normal and there's abnormal. Aaron seemed preoccupied with promoting his own image to an abnormal extreme.

Part of the image was the desire to be seen as the "best with the best." He wanted other men to think he had the best wife, son, daughter, house, car, clothes, toys, and job of all his contemporaries. Even higher up the list, he wanted others to see him as a man of great integrity—almost perfection. He wanted every part of his observable life to reek of quality, high ideals, and near-flawless spirituality.

When you observed Susan, that's what you got. For her it wasn't an act. She was a mature, godly woman. Her life merely reflected what she was deep in her heart.

Aaron, on the other hand, came across not so much as a godly person but as someone play-acting the script of a godly person. His preoccupation with having people perceive him this way didn't ring true with me. He seemed like Pilate, repeatedly washing his hands, trying to convince himself that removing the dirt on the outside could remove the guilt on the inside. Aaron wanted everyone to be so confident of his relationship with God that they would *assume* he was a man of integrity.

That was and is, of course, flawed thinking. The key to integrity is that who you are in public aligns with who you are in private, and that both public and private life align with God's standards. True integrity allows a few chosen individuals deep enough into one's private life so that they can compare the two life-styles and see they're equal. That's the kind of accountability that makes integrity pure.

No one had access to Aaron's private life. Not even his wife. And when I occasionally ventured close to the shadows of his hidden life, I noticed his strong commitment to image control the most.

What's Image Control?

What I call "image control" happens when a person creates an illusion about who he is and then gets everyone, including himself, to accept the illusion as real. Once the person creating the illusion has adequately convinced himself, his heart gets fogged with ambivalence, guilt, and worry. Deep down inside, something tells him he's a walking lie.

Aaron used high-control to maintain his masquerade. He forced the people close to him to pay strict attention to the facade. He controlled their social contacts, the choice of their spiritual mentors, and as many of the rest of the facets of their lives as he could. At first, Susan didn't find his manipulative tendencies or his aggressive personality that oppressive, simply because it was directed at maintaining a high standard she already embraced. But if she could have known what he was doing behind her back, she would have seen his manipulative, overbearing emotions for what they were—a mask to hide his private addictions.

Not until the afternoon when she showed up unexpectedly and caught him involved in one of his addictions did she get her first clue that he might be keeping a big part of his life from her. In the months that followed her discovery, she found Aaron's life was tied up in knots—his private life was layer upon layer of self-destructive addictions. She found drugs, pornography, sexual liaisons, and habitual lies he had been telling to his employer and her. All this had been going on right under her nose for years. She had been clueless.

Putting all the pieces together made her start to see his overbearing personality differently. As she evaluated incidents—even conflicts—of the past, she suddenly saw the pattern that had enabled Aaron to keep his secret life so effectively hidden.

Then came "the mother of all counseling appointments," and I was chosen to be the counselor. The two of them had come to the point that if something drastic didn't happen to rebuild Susan's confidence in Aaron, their marriage would be through. Aaron needed to come clean—with himself, with God, and with his wife.

Susan had fled their home for a few days to try to gain some objectivity. Aaron suggested this counseling session. He wanted to gain back his wife and children. He hope to salvage the little bit of hope remaining for his family. We had counted down to this day, but even in this "coming out" session, he insisted on setting the bulk of the agenda—where, when, with whom, and so on. In other words, he wanted to control.

Aaron spent about an hour talking vaguely around the problem—another controlling tactic. He drew heavily from the catalog of wonderful memories he and Susan had accumulated and used them to remind her of the deep sincerity with which he had always loved her—control. His eyes twinkled as he recalled incidents with his children—choking up over the level of his devotion to them—control. He mentioned only surface sins that, he assured her, he was getting over—control.

"Aaron, let's get on with it," I finally said. "You've come here to seek peace with God. You're evading Him and avoiding the purpose of this meeting that *you* called. C'mon, it's time to stop hiding."

There was a pregnant pause as he looked down at his feet. Tears welled up in his eyes, and he started to whisper obscenities. The most vulgar expressions in the English language started coming out from somewhere below his soul. Then came the explosion. He jumped to his feet, turned to the wall beside him, and delivered four fierce blows. Three went directly through the drywall, and one smashed into a picture hanging to the right of him. The glass shattered throughout the room, and blood shot from his hand. In a single move, he broke the leg off a chair and smashed some knickknacks on the shelf behind him. Then he slumped back against the wall, slid slowly down to the carpet, and started to wail from deep within. And in that humiliated state of contrition, Aaron took his first steps from the dungeon of bondage to the bright light of freedom.

Rolling the Dice with the Devil

Aaron had *fear*, Aaron had *rage*, and Aaron was fraught with *shame*. But there was one additional element that made him such a slave to those three internal enemies that he could do nothing on his own to get clear of them. Aaron had allowed Satan to build a fortress in his soul.

I'm not talking about demon possession. Too often, the devil is used as a scapegoat for the lack of human responsibility. Aaron wasn't possessed— he was *oppressed*. Because of a series of unfortunate choices, he was allowing himself to be tied and gagged by the powers of darkness.

What's the difference between possession and oppression? Aaron hadn't made a pact with the devil; he'd just played a few hands of poker with him—and lost. From early in his childhood, Aaron had been undisciplined about the influences he allowed into his life. He hung around places and people that took their cues from the father of lies— Satan. And little by little, Satan encroached upon Aaron's life until he held a poisonous position of leverage in his heart.

There was no doubt about his belief in Jesus Christ. The problem was that his track record throughout childhood, his teen years, and his young adult life left him without any confidence that God's love could work *in him*. It wasn't God he doubted but himself. Every time he prayed and asked God to take away his shame, Satan faxed him a lie.

"Forgive you? Ha! You've slipped through the back door of too many massage parlors, buddy. Face it, you're hooked—and you *like* it that way. You know that whatever action you take, it'll be short-lived. God's grace only works for those strong enough to live out His Word. You don't have it in you, Aaron, so quit trying."

Every time Aaron asked God to lift his oppressive rage, the lies began. As for fear, Satan simply used against him the fear that was already choking Aaron's heart. As a result, for decades Aaron had felt paralyzed.

Button-Holing Bondage

Fear, rage, and shame fuel a high-control personality. In the context of a normal Christian environment, they can be dealt with effectively by appropriating the power God makes available to the willing heart. Satan may try to influence a person, but his access to that person's life is in direct proportion to the invitations he's received to enter in. A conscientious Christian is normally careful about his contact with people and places where Satan already has a stronghold.

Fear, anger, and shame can turn into spiritual bondage if we aren't careful, however. Knowing how this can happen is the first key to stopping it from happening. The Bible teaches that temptation confronts us through three corridors:

- the world system (our corrupted surroundings)
- the flesh (our selfish desires)
- the devil

In many high-control personalities, the battles against freedom are being fought somewhere in the first two corridors—the world system and the flesh. To put ourselves in bondage to either of these two areas of temptation, we simply have to make a *series* of wrong choices. After a while, our choices bring our wills into a state of passivity. They stop screening the temptations, weighing them against God's Word, and claiming His power over them. After a while, sin from the world or the flesh has us by the throat, and we feel powerless to overcome it.

A teenage couple might be committed to Christ and desire to honor Him in their dating life. But let's say that on one of their dates, their passions get the best of them, and they surrender to their urges. Normally this is followed by a sense of guilt, maybe shame, and repentance (we hope). They ask God to forgive them and make some decisions about guarding their purity in the future. However, a month later, they surrender again to the urges of their flesh. Once again, there's guilt and repentance. But the intensity of both the guilt and the repentance has changed. It's not as strong as the first time. Two weeks later, they have sex again. Then four days later. Then...they're hooked. They're in bondage to the flesh, and they feel too weak to utilize God's power to overcome their bondage. All it took was a series of wrong choices.

When we add the third area of temptation into the mix—the devil—the slide into bondage is complete. Satan wants more than a foothold; he wants to erect a fortress within our volition. When we allow him access to our minds, he changes the playing field and the rules. And he wields significant power to distort our view of ourselves, as well as our view of God.

Most people, when asked to describe how they view the conflict between God and Satan, picture themselves being pulled back and forth between two gigantic forces. Actually, one Force is unfathomable in size, power, love, and grace. The other is merely a gnat *with a big mouth*—but he uses it effectively.

Christ's power over Satan, according to the Scriptures, is total and not to be questioned. But Satan's power over people is another matter. When he is granted (either willingly or through naiveté) a place in our lives, he wields incredible influence over our decisions. When we've fallen into his bondage, the urge to control other people is a natural by-product. In addition, he takes advantage of any surrendering we've already done to the world system or our flesh. When we're in this state of defenselessness, he can devour us for dinner.

Bondage, therefore, is the outgrowth of wrong choices that enable Satan to manipulate our fear, anger, and shame to such a degree that we feel powerless to overcome them or him. Often, it's in this internal climate that addictions grow. They can be countless. On the one side, we have the unacceptable addictions: drugs, alcohol, sex, various eating disorders. On the other side we have a myriad of "acceptable" or "respected" addictions: workaholism, perfectionism, materialism, churchaholism. These addictions line up in the back of our brains and march through our daily lives, demanding that we keep step with their cadence.

Bondage insists that we control the people around us. If we don't, we leave ourselves vulnerable to their scrutiny and rejection. The last thing people in bondage want is to be found out. So they work overtime to control those close to them in order to avoid the pain that goes with confronting their bondage.

If a woman is in bondage to her social status, for instance, she feels a strong compulsion to control the tastes and actions of those close to her, lest they somehow undermine her status. Suppose her daughter brings a friend from the wrong side of the tracks to their upwardly mobile suburban home. The mother, intoxicated with making proper social statements, may make a series of comments or moves that attack the relationship between her daughter and the friend. She may carp on the friend's weaknesses or make comparisons between her daughter's proper grooming and her friend's unsophisticated style. She may forbid them to see each other or try to arrange a friendship from a more "acceptable" family.

As parents, we have a responsibility to help our children make wise choices about their friends. We do *not* have the right before God to encourage them to withhold kindness or friendship from a person simply because that person doesn't meet our ego-motivated, superficial standards.

If we're in bondage to money, we may push people to make purchases that are not in the best interests of anyone. A spouse may whine, complain, or connive against a partner to get that person to produce more income, and the deeply imbedded motivation isn't stewardship but greed. It doesn't take long for the spouse to feel used and abused. Many working mothers feel they are working simply because their husbands refuse to curb their wants. Husbands can't finance their expensive tastes on their income alone, so they push their wives out of their role as homemaker in order to shore up the family's faltering financial nightmare. These husbands may be in so much bondage to their flesh that they feel too paralyzed to do anything about it.

"The Devil Made Me Do It"

Satan is blamed for a lot of things for which he isn't responsible—and he loves it every time. It propagates myths about his strength and frees him to gain greater control in areas where he truly *is* responsible. People can be in bondage to Satan and not know it; they could even be pastoring churches in the process! Many pastors who have fallen into satanic quicksand can testify to how subtle his ways are.

One pastor found himself in bondage to Satan's schemes as a result of doing an in-depth study on the ways of the devil without simultaneously being careful to maintain a strong relationship with God through prayer, praise, confession, Bible reading, and accountability. He was doing research for a book he was writing about Satan. In the process, he exposed himself to a lot of the overt occult exercises that people of the dark side embrace. His research took him on Satan's trail through the back alleys where drugs, pimps, prostitutes, and violence thrive. He was naive about Satan's techniques and took his power for granted.

Eventually, the trap snapped shut on him. His countenance fell, his personality shifted, his teaching became less reliable, he became undependable to his family and friends, his mood shifted into a more explosive attitude, and he became obsessed with keeping people clear of his private research. He assured his wife that he could handle it. In addition, he insisted on her helping him cover his problems by defending him to the flock. But when you're in bondage to Satan, he eventually brings you down. It took losing his wife, his ministry, and his reputation before he came to his senses enough to claim Christ's power.

Enemies in the Camp

High-control tendencies are one of the biggest tip-offs to bondage in a person's life. The bondage may grow out of fear, anger, or shame, but it nevertheless gains such a hold that the bound person can't seem to do anything about it.

When our children become more sophisticated in their manipulation, it could be pointing to some major strongholds Satan has gained in their lives. They may be listening to destructive music or watching harmful movies. Aaron, whose story was told at the beginning of this chapter, found that Satan got the first hold on his life when he viewed the movie *The Exorcist* in junior high school! Sometimes it's little more than one of our children's friends who is involved in a cult that gives Satan a foothold in our kids' lives.

Some of the best work done on this subject is by Dr. Neil Anderson of Freedom in Christ Ministries.[1] I recommend reading his book *The Bondage*

Breaker. It develops the ways Satan gets a foothold in a person's life, thereby building a fortress within that person's family. I also recommend a book Anderson co-authored with youth evangelist Steve Russo entitled *The Seduction of Our Children*. Both of these books are balanced works on this often-confusing issue of Satan and the human heart.

In an accompanying workbook, Anderson provides a list of ways Satan can gain a foothold in our loved ones' lives. Here are some of them:

- Ouija board
- table lifting
- fortune telling
- amateur hypnosis
- rod and pendulum (dowsing)
- palm reading
- spirit guides
- mental suggestions (or attempting to swap mental thoughts)
- astrology
- ghosts
- seances
- tarot cards
- magic eight ball

These are only some of the practices on his list. Most of the ones listed here are the subject matter or props of many movies directed toward our children or teenagers. Sometimes well-meaning but naive parents actually pick up these videos for their kids to watch. They don't realize they are handing their kids' minds over to be tutored by the father of lies. After enough exposure to this kind of material, children's behavior changes. Others in the family begin to have feelings of being held hostage. At this point, parents must take some deliberate spiritual steps.

Besides the practices listed above, contact with cults can also bring family members into satanic bondage. A husband might be transferred into a department at work with a supervisor who's heavily into a high-control cult. He might even find a supervisor who delves into the occult. Unless he's prepared to wear the full armor of God,[2] he could find himself losing more and more battles with the world, the flesh, and the devil—even though he wants nothing to do with that cult.

Without realizing it, we could be setting up our family relationships for emotional friendly fire—high-control wounds administered by people within the family circle. These wounds leave victims with emotional scar tissue that never goes away. The keys to helping a high-control person are to make sure we're aware of ways he might be in bondage, and then to take the necessary steps to bring freedom to his heart.

Don't Get Fenced In

The life of faith is the only real life of freedom. When we put our confidence in God and refuse to "lean on our own understanding," we turn our back on bondage. But if we're already "hooked," we need to get big-league help. For most people, it's a prayer away. Others may need to utilize the help of a pastor or competent counselor. If it's a child who is struggling, you might want to seek help from pros like Neil Anderson's ministry, which I mentioned above.

My purpose in this chapter has been to show how bondage can cause high-control behavior—whether the bondage comes through the world system, the flesh, or the devil. Later we'll look at steps that can be used to free the controller as well as the controlled person. For now, I want to close our discussion of bondage with a few verses from God's Word that assure us He can enable us to be freed from our bondages.

Paul referred to our ability to get drawn into bondage, even after we've given our lives to Christ, when he said:

> *It was for freedom that Christ set us free; therefore keep standing firm and do not be subject again to a yoke of slavery.*
> Galatians 5:1

In that verse, he was referring to the bondage of legalism (the antithesis of grace). He made it clear that for us to avoid bondage, we have a responsibility—we're to stand firm. In another passage, he told us how unresolved anger can lead to bondage:

> *Be angry, and yet do not sin; do not let the sun go down on your anger, and do not give the devil an opportunity.*
> Ephesians 4:26-27

Once again, we see there is some responsibility on our part. If we don't want Satan to gain a foothold, we must make sure we don't make a series of poor choices when it comes to our anger. As we've seen, anger is one of the primary methods of controlling. A reconciled set of emotions keeps Satan from establishing a beachhead in our hearts.

Let me point out one more passage from the apostle Paul in which he urged us to surrender all parts of our being to the ownership and control of Christ in order to avoid falling into bondage:

> *But examine everything carefully; hold fast to that which is good; abstain from every form of evil. Now may the God of peace Himself sanctify you entirely; and may your spirit and soul and body be preserved complete, without blame at the coming of our Lord Jesus Christ.*
>
> I Thessalonians 5:21-23

We can have victory over the bondage that drives us to control the people we love. We can also have victory over the world, the flesh, and the devil. God's Word speaks about each of these three areas of temptation. Regarding the world:

> *These things I have spoken to you, that in Me you may have peace. In the world you have tribulation, but take courage; I have overcome the world.*
>
> John 16:33

> *For whatever is born of God overcomes the world; and this is the victory that has overcome the world—our faith.*
>
> 1 John 5:4

Regarding the flesh:

> *For we are the true circumcision, who worship in the Spirit of God and glory in Christ Jesus, and place no confidence in the flesh.*
>
> Philippians 3:3

Regarding the devil:

Submit therefore to God. Resist the devil and he will flee from you.
James 4:7

God wants to bring freedom to the relationships within His family. High control undermines all He is trying to do to us and through us.

In these last four chapters, we've looked at four toxic causes of high-control personalities—fear, rage, shame, and bondage. In the next chapter, we'll consider the final cause of high-control tendencies. Different from the first four, this cause is rooted in the areas of our lives where God has truly gifted us. I call this powerful yet hard-to-perceive problem *toxic strength*.

CHAPTER 11

Toxic Strength

There's a cliché I'm sure you've heard: "You don't know your own strength." Usually the statement refers to our physical capabilities. You might be trying to have fun with someone and end up playing too rough. I've done that before, and I've had it done to me. When you're physically strong, it's sometimes difficult to gauge the tolerance threshold of the people around you.

That's why I get on my back and automatically assume the "pinned" position when I'm wrestling my three-year-old son. That's why I start with four letters against me when I'm shooting a game of "horse" on a basketball court with my 12-year-old daughter.

If people know they don't stand a chance from the beginning, all ambition is sucked out of their spirits. So if one of the purposes of a family is to bring out the best in each member, we need to keep our strengths under control.

That's what I watch the guys do to the horses out at the Douglas Ranch. You've never been there, I suppose, but if you had, you'd meet my friend Dennis. He ranches several sections of high desert—running cattle on his land for nine months each year. He and his fellow cowboys use a lot of horses to move the herds around. They harness their horses' strength—literally. The bridles, saddles, and spurs help leverage the horses' power so they can accomplish their purposes. Within our homes, the values, convictions, and disciplines we live by help harness the strength of our families as a whole. They keep us focused and on course.

But this type of harness assumes that everyone is cooperative. I wish that were the case. The painful truth, however, is that the corporate strength of a family depends on the level of commitment of each member toward disciplining his or her personal strengths. It's like the headlights on your car. They have two levels of brightness. You put them on high beam when you're either leading the pack or you have the road all to yourself. But when you encounter someone else approaching at a distance, you're supposed to dim your lights to low beam. If you don't, you'll blind the other driver and make it difficult for him to stay safely on the road.

A guy in a Volkswagen can force the oncoming driver of a dump truck to lose control of his vehicle, simply by forgetting (or refusing) to dim his headlights. Kids on high beams can run their parents' emotions off course, too. A husband who refuses to turn down his natural and innate strength a few notches can drive his wife into an emotional canyon.

That brings up the subject matter at hand. I've entitled this chapter "Toxic Strength" as my way of capsulizing and defining a phenomenon that plagues many families who live with a high controller in their midst. Different from the four root causes we've discussed in the previous chapters, toxic strength is based on a good thing that is poorly managed.

Aristotle and the Four Dwarfs

Several thousand years ago, the best thinkers of the Greek culture sat on their marble slabs discussing the mysteries of the human mind. Within that ancient think tank, some conclusions were drawn about how we are emotionally wired; their insights have endured the scrutiny of time. One of their most famous professors, Aristotle, was the first person credited with dividing personalities into four quadrants, or styles, of human personality that make up the bulk of the population. Most people are born with one of these styles as their dominant "bent." Obviously, every person has traces or degrees of the other styles as well. We're hybrids with one or sometimes two of the styles being the one(s) we act out of the most. But for the most part, one style dominates each personality.

Of course, some people automatically resist this kind of personality analysis. They complain that it "labels" or "pigeonholes" individuals and distills them down to a simple checklist. They complain that it locks people into a view of themselves and determines behavior. (I've never known any checklist, however, that is capable of altering a person's fundamental personality style.)

Sometimes critics point out the flaws in this type of personality categorizing by showing that they "test out" with one personality style at home and a different style in the workplace. Actually, that's to be expected. As a person who oversees a company, I have to lean heavily on a secondary personality style at the office while I function far more in my primary style at home.

Criticism aside, the historical record demonstrates that Aristotle did his homework. He accurately identified the four basic styles of human personality.[1]

For our discussion here, I want to give each personality style a descriptive name that will help you understand its most obvious characteristics. I'll list six ways in which each style demonstrates itself. Then we're going to take them to Disneyland!

Fearless: "Let's Do It Now!"
1. Fearless people lead, whether you want them to or not! They're notorious for making plans on others' behalf.
2. Fearless people thrive on confrontation, competition, and pressure. Those things let them test their capabilities. The greater the odds stacked against them, the better.
3. Fearless people have no difficulty making decisions. They'll make all the decisions pertaining to their lives—and all those pertaining to yours if you let them. They can't fathom how you could think anything except that their plan is the best.
4. Fearless people don't mince words. If you're going to converse with them, you might want to save the flowery orations for someone else.
5. Fearless people like quick results. Their favorite time frame is now!
6. Fearless people don't give up easily. They are enterprising, determined, and daring. Once they know what they want, it's hard to distract them.

Spontaneous: "Trust Me, We'll Make It!"
1. Spontaneous people are parties looking for a place to happen. More than anything, they just want to have fun.
2. Spontaneous people can't wait to see what's just over the horizon. They give the word *visionary* its meaning.
3. Spontaneous people love the sound of their own voices. Enough said.
4. Spontaneous people wake up smiling. They are civilization's "born optimists."
5. Spontaneous people never read the directions. The fine print bores them.
6. Spontaneous people can mobilize and motivate others with ease. They love to build people up and help their dreams come true.

Loyal: "Let's Not Change Anything, Okay?"
1. Loyal people are great listeners. This enables them to accommodate their need for close relationships.
2. Loyal people are emotional first-aid kits. They are innately compassionate.
3. Loyal people love to please their peers. Conflict intimidates them. They are notorious for saying yes to every idea or request from their friends. "Do you want to go bowling?" "Sure!" "Do you want to stay up all night?" "Sure!" "Could you do my homework for me?" "Sure!"
4. Loyal people are intensely sensitive. They're tenacious friends— overwhelmingly thoughtful.
5. Loyal people can put up with a lot. They are uniquely gifted with the ability to love the one they're with. Although they despise change, they are such strong people pleasers that they'll grit their teeth and bear it.
6. Loyal people don't compromise the things that really matter to them. They stubbornly hold on to what they feel is right.

Deliberate: "Wait While I Read the Directions."
1. Deliberate people guard their hearts. They are often difficult to

read because they conceal their emotions.

2. Deliberate people go by the book. They read the owner's manual and hate to deviate from the plan. One of their favorite sayings is "Let's do it correctly."

3. Deliberate people hate change. If it's not part of the original plan, forget it.

4. Deliberate people stuff their anger. To show it would be to expose their hearts too much. They'd rather suffer in silence than fight.

5. Deliberate people love to solve problems. It enables them to use their vast analytical skills.

6. Deliberate people ask lots of questions. They're never satisfied with how much they know.

Fearless, spontaneous, loyal, and deliberate. We'd love to be all of them, and at times we try. But as life drops its pop quizzes on us, we usually find that we grade high on one, average on two, and flunk the fourth miserably. That's nothing to be ashamed of. God designed us that way. It's His way of showing us how much we need each other...and Him.

Reality dictates that one person's strength will inevitably bring out the worst in the next guy. When the people we're talking about happen to gather around our dinner table every night, we don't have to look far to see why God sent us a Savior. Strengths become weaknesses when pushed to extremes. And when a person is determined to have his own way, regardless of how it affects the people close to him, family members will find themselves fighting for position. The fifth reason people control, therefore, is often a case of naiveté. They don't realize their own strength, and they fail to honor and guard the uniqueness of others.

"It's a Small World After All"

Now let's take those four personality styles to Disneyland and see how they respond to different situations. The first two, Fearless and Spontaneous, tend to control people. The second two, Loyal and Deliberate, tend to try to control their environment. So it's off to the Magic Kingdom to see what happens when we drop them at the front gate for a day in the "land of enchantment."

Fearless jumps out of the van first and takes off for the turnstile without waiting to see if anybody needs help. That's Loyal's job. She's making sure everyone has his jacket, fanny pack, and number 30 sun block. Spontaneous climbs out of the van and notices a bus load of tourists unloading directly behind him. With his feet tapping to the background music from the park, he shakes hands with all the people as they disembark, welcoming them to Main Street U.S.A. Deliberate buys the tickets, carefully counting the change and marking down this first expense on his pocket notebook.

Loyal pulls Spontaneous toward the turnstile as he waves good-bye to the people milling around the bus. She turns him around as she approaches the turnstile—just in time for him to introduce himself to the man waiting to take his ticket. As Deliberate meets up with the group, Fearless grabs a ticket out of his hand and asks what took him so long. When Deliberate doesn't reply, Fearless elbows his way to the front of the group so that he can get through the gates first.

Inside the park, Loyal wants to take a picture of everyone in front of the floral Mickey Mouse. Spontaneous takes the center position. Deliberate asks if she made sure she set the ASA on the camera to the corresponding ASA on the film. Fearless checks his watch, mumbles something under his breath, and then recruits a passerby to take the snapshot. Loyal gets behind them and wraps her arms around all three.

Just inside the town square, the group encounters Mickey and Minnie Mouse surrounded by guests. "Look," says Spontaneous. "There are the Disney mice. Let me stop by and introduce myself." While Spontaneous shakes Mickey's hand, Loyal helps all the others get close enough for a good picture with Mickey.

Meanwhile, Fearless is marching down the middle of Main Street, unaware that no one is following him. Deliberate stands by the band shell, carefully studying the park map. He numbers the attractions in the order he thinks the quartet should see them and calculates the approximate time that they should be getting to each location.

So it goes all day long. Fearless leads the way, always far ahead of the others. Spontaneous tells jokes to strangers as they wait in line. Deliberate keeps track of how much money they're spending. And Loyal has a great time just listening and generally taking care of everyone.

Harnessing Your Potential

You can probably tell I've been to Disneyland a few times. What's more germane to our discussion here is that I've actually followed those four personalities around. Colt is our Fearless leader. Karis is the Spontaneous entertainment who keeps us amused while standing in line. (She's also a clone of yours truly.) Cody is our Deliberate computer, making sure we don't miss anything we planned. Shiloh is our Loyal caretaker who works her magic on us late in the day when our feet are tired and our patience is shot. (She takes after her mom.) I love each of them for who they are and for the strength they bring to our family circle.

You have composites of these personalities slipping in and out of your life, too. They are the sum total of your waking hours—the bottom line of your stated purpose as a parent and a spouse. They may also be the main reason you purchased this book. You couldn't love them more than you do, but the coercion you experience from the strength of their personalities sometimes makes you wish you'd stayed single. Or maybe you are single and you, too, encounter your share of people whose natural strengths slip over the line of acceptance.

Don't panic. We all feel that way at times. Although all of us have strengths that can turn into tools for overcontrol, God has a way to give us victory in the midst of the battle.

A Walk in the Right Direction

We've discussed the ways we control each other, and we've discussed the reasons. In the final chapters, we're going to learn the principles that free the vital relationships within the family and help bring the best out of each person. Take a walk with me—past the silhouette of the cross and beyond the empty tomb—and bask with me in the warm rays of God's grace. We'll study the principles that break the bonds of control in your family and help you empower the people you love to be all God intended them to be.

Part Four

CHAPTER 12

Grace-Based Families

I t was a packed flight to Dallas. One of the attendants was closing the front door of our DC-10, while another told us over the intercom to take our seats. Only a handful of empty seats remained on the jumbo jetliner, and I was quietly enjoying my good fortune of having one of them next to me. With an aisle on one side and an empty seat between me and the window, I could stretch out my legs and spread out my work for the duration of the flight.

I was too busy unpacking some files from my briefcase to notice the flight attendant reopening the door to let a lone, late passenger on board. Just when I got myself "moved in," I noticed the woman, loaded down with carry-on baggage, standing next to me. She was looking at her boarding pass and the number printed above my row.

"That's my seat," she said, nodding to the one where I had just stacked my files and books. As I got up to make room for her and all her stuff, the cliché about counting chickens before they're hatched rattled around in my head! She had an oversized purse, a large tote bag filled with magazines, a long set of blueprints, and a portfolio case (the kind graphic artists carry), as well as her coat. I popped open a few of the overhead compartments but couldn't find one with any space for her stuff.

"That's okay," she told me, "I'll fit it all in here."

Wonderful, I thought. *It will be a tight trip to Big D.* I decided it would be too difficult to do any paperwork in the little space that was left, so I took out a book and was deep into its plot when we reached our cruising altitude. The seat belt lights went off, the beverage service began, and my fellow passengers were relaxing from the quiet tension that always seems to accompany takeoff.

I had not spoken to the woman next to me since she sat down, and I was so much into the book I was reading that I scarcely noticed she was there. Then it started.

I barely noticed it at first. It was faint, almost imperceptible, when it began. But as my eyes danced down the paragraphs of my book, my subconscious picked up the subtle sounds coming from the seat next to me. It sounded like a gerbil nesting. Paper tearing. Paper crumpling. More tearing paper. Scratching.

I glanced to the left. Her hands were busy. The stack of magazines was about six inches high. The way she snipped at the pages with her scissors made it obvious she'd done this before. A lot. My fellow passenger was leafing through the magazines, stopping every few pages to cut out a picture, and then filing it in an accordion folder she balanced on her knees. I noticed that all the pictures were of the interior of beautiful houses.

"Are you an architect?" I asked.

She didn't notice I was asking her a question until I asked it a second time.

"Excuse me?" she said.

"The pictures you're cutting out—are you an architect or an interior designer?"

"Oh, this stuff. No, I'm a makeup artist. I'm cutting these out because my husband and I are building a house, and I just want some more ideas for the inside."

From the size of her stack, I figured I might as well get used to the (irritating) sound of her snipping away. I went back to reading my book.

The beverage service came, and I pulled my tray table down so the attendant could put my coffee on something solid. It wasn't there a minute before the lady next to me caught it with the corner of one of her magazines and dumped its entire contents in my lap. I'd picked a bad day to travel in my off-white slacks. They were a mess. My seat was soaked. And I gritted my teeth from the scalding heat and personal humiliation. I'd save the feelings of embarrassment for when I had to walk through the Dallas airport in my "outfit."

The lady was genuinely sorry. These things happen. I prefer that they happen to someone else, but that day, it just seemed to be my turn. There was nothing I could do about my predicament, so I decided to make the best of a lousy situation. When a stranger dumps hot coffee all over you, it's easy to strike up a conversation and get acquainted. She was so relieved I wasn't hostile that she proceeded to converse with me as if we'd known each other since college.

Two things seemed to be her overriding obsessions: the house she and her husband were building, and the faces of some of Hollywood's most famous people for whom she had done makeup. She was just returning from prepping a star for a photo session. Without asking if I was interested, she got out her portfolio and showed me some of the faces she had made beautiful over the years. As soon as I saw some of them, I was definitely interested. These were the people of *People* magazine—the box-office big shots who crowd the front cover of tabloids at the checkout stand. She had her own version of the inside stories.

After breakfast, she insisted on showing me the blueprints for her new home. During the summers between my college and graduate-school years, I had worked with construction crews building both residential and commercial buildings. I knew enough about construction to intelligently read blueprints and ask decent questions. She and her husband were building a magnificent house—most people would consider it a mansion. I was musing that makeup artists must make more money than I thought when she volunteered that her husband was an orthopedic surgeon. Then the elaborate blueprints made more sense.

"There's lots of bedrooms," I noticed out loud.

"We've got lots of kids. It's the second marriage for both of us. He had three, I have two. Plus, I'm three months pregnant with our first. The nursery is going to go right here." She pointed to a room just off the master suite.

"Congratulations," I said, picturing all those kids, in this huge house, with this pregnant woman down in the family room, snipping pictures out of magazines. There's something about the calling of ordained minister that causes you to ask questions that are technically none of your business. So I asked, "How do you manage so many kids and travel to so many movie locations?"

That's when I learned about the string of nannies she'd been through; the anxiety she feels when she's trying to coordinate the kids' schedules from a distance; and the pressure all of this has put on her marriage. Her career cost her first marriage (her words), but she refused to alter anything in her life. She loved the glitter, glamour, and paparazzi that surrounded the beautiful people. "Besides," she said, "I don't get along that well with his kids."

I learned, without asking, that her first marriage had been plagued by years of arguing over career goals and children. Her present relationship wasn't going as well as she would have preferred. Her doctor-husband was seldom there, and when he was, he barked orders at everyone as though he were still in the operating room. The two sets of kids weren't blending well, either. I asked if she'd gotten the kids involved in a good church.

"Sunday's the only day I have for myself. My husband's two oldest kids go to their church, but I usually sleep in and then take my two kids out to breakfast."

I flipped through the blueprints to the page dedicated to the foundation. Most home builders don't spend much time studying it. The architect had gone to painstaking lengths to detail the elaborate specifications needed to hold up such a magnificent house. Even my amateur knowledge could tell that the concrete and rebar these blueprints called for were going to cost more than the average homeowner spends on his entire house.

"That's quite a foundation," I remarked.

"What?"

"The foundation. It's very complicated. Plan on the builders spending quite a while putting it in."

"I don't know anything about foundations. On this project, I only concern myself with what I can see."

It was the obvious truth, not just about the house's foundation, but about her personal life as well. As I watched her roll up the blueprints and snap the rubber band around them, I wondered if she would get that house in her next divorce settlement. (I would have thought that whether she had dumped coffee in my lap or not.)

It's Not What Meets the Eye

The psalmist said that "*Unless the Lord builds the house, they labor in vain who build it*" (Psalm 127:1a). We've been learning about high-control relationships within families that deflate people's view of themselves and limit their potential. We've learned the techniques that controllers use and the reasons they use them. In this last section, we want to gain freedom for our families. As we shift gears to look at some practical steps we can take to release vital relationships from the bondage of high control, it's imperative that we talk about the foundation these freed-up relationships must be built upon. One word says it—**grace.**

Grace is a five-letter word that contains the essence of God's plan for the ages. As the hymnist so poetically said, we need "grace that is greater than all our sin." From the beginning of time, God's relationship with mankind has been the story of His grace being bestowed on the undeserving. Even during the oppressive centuries when the prevailing relationship between humanity and God came through the strict limitations of Mosaic law, His grace was at work, leading people out of darkness and into His light.

Three things have existed from the first week of creation to the present, and they will continue to exist long after this world is destroyed. They are:
1. God
2. His Word
3. Families

Leaders come and go. Economies come and go. Governments come and go. But God, His Word, and families string their way through the comings and goings of time. I guess that's why I'm so concerned about what goes on within the family circle, and why I've spent my adult life studying this subject. I agree with Chuck Swindoll when he says, "Home is where life makes up its mind." So much of life is determined by the climate and character of our families.

We do not live in a grace-based world. We're surrounded by oppression, selfishness, power brokers, and myriad impositions. Our heavily armed defense department is evidence of how much we feel we can trust the countries surrounding us. God wants to shed His grace on us. The best vehicle for Him to use is a family in which relationships are held together by unconditional love. I call these types of homes grace-based families. They're the antithesis of high control.

Mary Had a Little Lamb

The Lord Jesus grew up in a grace-based home. We see evidence of that in an interesting anecdote from his childhood. It's found in the second chapter of Luke. The last few verses relate an incident that took place when His family made its annual trip to Jerusalem to celebrate the Passover.

This Passover trip was special for Jesus, for it was the year he turned 12. That's a benchmark year for a Jewish boy, marking the end of childhood and the beginning of the transition into adult independence.

After the Passover celebration, when the caravan pulled away from the city, Mary and Joseph assumed Jesus was with his cousin John and his parents. If He wasn't with them, maybe He was with some of the many acquaintances traveling with them. When He didn't show up at their campfire for dinner, however, they became concerned. When he was nowhere to be found, they doubled back to Jerusalem.

It took them three days to locate Him. He was in the temple, sitting among the wisest rabbis of his day, both listening and asking questions. The teachers were amazed at His understanding and His answers to their questions.

Have you ever lost one of your kids? Even if it's just for five minutes at the mall, it's a frightening predicament. You hope for the best while dreading the worst, and you can't relax until you have that child safely back under your care. When you finally locate the child, you have two emotions colliding within. On the one hand, you're relieved that he's okay. But at the same time, you're frustrated (angry) with him for wandering off and scaring you so badly. Jesus' parents were no different from you and me.

Look at Luke 2:48-49: *"And when they saw Him, they were astonished; and His mother said to Him, 'Son, why have You treated us this way? Behold, Your father and I have been anxiously looking for You.'"*

Jesus had an interesting reply for a 12-year-old: *"He said to them, 'Why is it that you were looking for Me? Did you not know that I had to be in My Father's house?' "*

Let me paraphrase what I think He was saying: "Mom and Dad, we sent you angels. Remember? We sent one to each of you, and they explained to you that I am different and have come to earth for a specific purpose. Now I'm fulfilling that purpose."

The text goes on to say they didn't understand His statement. They knew He was special, and they knew He had a specific agenda, but they didn't think it included frightening them. It's good they didn't know what was just ahead. Barely 20 years later, Mary would walk to the top of a hill outside that same town and stand eye level to the bloody feet of this same boy who had frightened them so.

As you read the conclusion to this incident in the temple, it's easy to slip over it so fast that you miss one of the greatest lessons about the kind of parents Jesus had and the kind of son He was.

Look at verses 51-52: *"And He went down with them, and came to Nazareth; and He continued in subjection to them; and His mother treasured all these things in her heart. And Jesus kept increasing in wisdom and stature, and in favor with God and men."*

There's a lesson for us in what transpired after this incident. But there's an even bigger lesson in what *didn't* transpire. Had I been Joseph, I would have been tempted to ground Jesus until He was 16. "You nearly gave us both a heart attack, boy! Have you no respect for us?" They could have come down real hard on Him, but they didn't. They gave Him grace.

What about Jesus? After all, He was the Son of God. He was the One who, during His childhood, ultimately heard the prayers his mom and dad whispered toward heaven after they tucked Him in bed every night. He could have been angry. He could have pulled divine rank on them. He could have been resentful for their questioning of His agenda. He could have called them something disrespectful and stormed out of the temple in order to embarrass them. But He didn't. He gave them grace. The God who made the universe, submitted to their authority.

Jesus had a grace-based family. We read about it in John 1:14. *"And the Word became flesh, and dwelt among us, and we beheld His glory, glory as of the only begotten from the Father, full of* **grace** *and truth"* (emphasis added).

You can have a grace-based family, too. In fact, it's a biblical mandate. Look how the apostle Paul put it: *"According to the grace of God which was given to me, as a wise master builder I laid a foundation, and another is building upon it. But let each man be careful how he builds upon it"* (1 Corinthians 3:10).

In a time when children have to take a number to see their parents, when spouses fax each other love notes from their offices, and families are being threatened by the most value hostile culture since the 1920s, we need grace. Let me list four characteristics of grace-based families.

Grace-Based Families Give Each Other the Freedom to be Different

Home needs to be a place where individuality is considered sacred. When my wife, Darcy, and I were courting each other, we were amazed at how many interests we shared. Before we got married, for example, Darcy loved to watch football with me on television. She'd sit beside me for hours, taking in the sights and sounds of the NFL.

Darcy used to make her own clothes. Before we married, I loved to help her pin the fabric on one of her patterns and then carefully cut it out for her.

After we were married, I'd ask Darcy to sit beside me and watch a football game.

"Why?" she'd say.

"You love sports."

"What made you think I love sports?"

After we were married, Darcy would ask me to help her pin up a pattern and cut it out for her.

"Why?" I asked.

"You love to help me make clothes."

"What made you think I love to help you make clothes?"

You're thinking, *Did you two deliberately deceive each other before you were married?*

No. Before we were married, Darcy thought she liked to watch football with me, and I thought I liked to help her make clothes. After we were married, we found out that in reality, we were different. You see, before we were married, we were fishing—she for me and I for her. I learned as a little kid that when you fish, the best bait to put on the hook is what the fish likes, not what you like.

Once we landed each other, we discovered we had a lot of different interests. That's not so bad. One of the great myths plaguing people who are looking for a partner is that they need to find someone with whom they have a lot in common. Reality dictates that is simply not true. Some of the greatest marriages in history were between people who had wide differences in tastes and interests. But what they did share was a commitment to their love. (If you want to read a good book on this subject, pick up Chuck and Barb Snyder's *Incompatibility: Grounds for a Great Marriage.*)[1]

For a marriage to be strong, we need to grant our partners the freedom to live out their God-given uniqueness. For children to reach their maximum potential as adults, they need to experience a childhood environment that offers the freedom to live out their uniqueness as well. In other words, we need to give them room for their quirks. Often, in granting them this type of grace, we are also better equipped to identify their strengths. It may irritate us when a son keeps catching flies and pulling their wings off, but who knows that we don't have a future surgeon (or coroner) in our midst! Proverbs 22:6 says (my paraphrase): *"Train up a child (literally) according to his unique inner bents, and when he is old he will not depart from them."*

Grace-based families, therefore, empower their members by giving them the freedom to be different.

Grace-Based Families Give
Each Other the Freedom to Be Vulnerable

In homes built on grace, people don't have to wear masks. They can verbalize their doubts and fears. Their vulnerabilities and inadequacies can come to the surface without fear of their being attacked.

In my book *Homegrown Heroes: How to Raise Courageous Kids*,[2] I tell about a father who was so angry at his son for striking out in the crucial last play of his Little League game that he made him take off his uniform and strip down to his underwear in front all his friends while screaming that he "wasn't worthy to wear the uniform."

Had I been at that game, I would have been tempted to catch that father as he walked by the backstop, reach through one of the holes in the chain-link fence, grab him by the face, and ask, "Do you remember the day you were born? You don't? Well, I'm going to reenact it." At that point, I'd want to pull his entire body through that little hole in the fence.

People's emotions are fragile—especially those of children. Home has got to be a place where weakness and vulnerabilities are allowed to be expressed without it costing individuals their dignity. Spouses need to be able to voice their fears. Children need to be able to verbalize their insecurities. When we respond with understanding, affection, and affirming words, we create the best environment possible to turn weakness into strength.

After all, some of our weaknesses have been put in our lives so that we can learn to lean on God for help. That's what Paul found out when he asked Him to take away an infirmity that he felt made him less effective as one of God's servants. The Lord said no:

"'My grace is sufficient for you, for power is perfected in weakness.' Most gladly, therefore, I will rather boast about my weaknesses, that the power of Christ may dwell in me" (2 Corinthians 12:9).

Paul reminded us that grace is supposed to flavor the words we say to the people around us:

"Let your speech always be with grace, seasoned, as it were, with salt, so that you may know how you should respond to each person" (Colossians 4:6).

Grace-based families, therefore, allow family members to be different and vulnerable.

Grace-Based Families Give Each Other the Freedom to Be Honest

High controllers are notorious for squelching the open exchange of feelings among family members. But families held together by grace allow people to vocalize what's in their hearts.

In the chapter entitled "Grace-Based Parenting," I'll offer a suggested forum for allowing children to voice their frustrations. It's a misunderstanding of respect and a misuse of authority to assert that children should never be allowed to speak up when their spirits are being crushed by one of their parents. Obviously, how children express themselves is important. Giving them an outlet for their anger doesn't mean they're free to dishonor us. But just as they occasionally exasperate us, we, likewise, exasperate them. Loving homes give enough grace to relationships so that those kinds of debilitating emotions don't have to back up in people's souls or plague them for years to come.

Legalistic homes are extremely high in control. They live by a Christian behavioral checklist rather than by faith. Once again, the apostle Paul comes to the family's rescue with a reminder about how grace should be the attitude of choice:

"Now therefore why do you put God to the test by placing upon the neck of the disciples a yoke which neither our fathers nor we have been able to bear? But we believe that we are saved through the grace of the Lord Jesus, in the same way as they also are" (Acts 15:10-11).

When we give our children and spouses an outlet to express their opinions and feelings, we empower them individually and increase the emotional health of our families. Grace, therefore, grants our loved ones a freedom to voice disappointments, even if *we* have disappointed them. The writer of the book of Hebrews told us what happens when we miss this opportunity to love by grace: *"See to it that no one comes short of the grace of God; that no root of bitterness springing up causes trouble, and by it many be defiled"* (Hebrews 12:15).

Grace-based families, therefore, allow each other to be different, vulnerable, and honest.

Grace-Based Families Give Each Other the Freedom to Be Wrong

If home is where life makes up its mind, then home must be a place where disappointments are tolerated, hurts are endured, and mistakes never mean the end of a relationship. Giving grace to people who have fallen short of God's glory doesn't mean we're condoning sinful behavior. Nor does it mean there are no consequences for the sin. But it does mean that those who have failed don't have to think their failure jeopardizes the rest of the family's commitment to them.

That's why God gave families the wonderful gift of forgiveness. Grace-based families exchange this gift among themselves—liberally. I'm not naive. I realize that some hurts to the heart are so severe that forgiveness seems impossible. But ultimately, it's what we are called to do.

To summarize, grace-based families give each other the freedom to be different, vulnerable, honest, and wrong.

The Foundation that Never Lets Us Fall

This is just one person's opinion, but I think the passage of Scripture that best outlines God's attitude about how we are to relate within our families is found in Philippians 2:1-8. That passage describes the kind of individual who refuses to be a vessel for high control. It's the pledge of allegiance of the grace-based heart:

> *If therefore there is any encouragement in Christ, if there is any consolation of love, if there is any fellowship of the Spirit, if any affection and compassion, make my joy complete by being of the same mind, maintaining the same love, united in spirit, intent on one purpose. Do nothing from selfishness or empty conceit, but with humility of mind let each of you regard one another as more important than himself; do not merely look out for your own personal interests, but also for the interests of others. Have this attitude in yourselves which was also in Christ Jesus, who, although He existed in the form of God, did not regard equality with God a thing to be grasped, but emptied Himself, taking the form of a bond-servant, and being made in the likeness of men. And being found in appearance as a man, He humbled Himself by becoming obedient to the point of death, even death on a cross.*

All of us are building our families on some kind of foundation. If it's a foundation that leverages one person's personality or position against another's weaknesses, we're not going to be very happy with what we end up building. If, on the other hand, we replace a foundation of control with one that is the best expression of God's heart—grace—we're going to like what's waiting for us as our families move through the different passages of time. The last verse of the last chapter of the last book of the Bible—the final message that came from the God who called Himself the Alpha and the Omega, who will have the last word—reinforces this point: *"The grace of the Lord Jesus be with all. Amen"* (Revelation 22:21).

God wants to permeate your family with grace. In the next chapter, we'll see specifically how to break the patterns of control by demonstrating grace with your spouse. That's where a grace-based foundation for your family begins. Help in establishing such a marriage is just a page away.

CHAPTER 13

Grace-Based Marriages

Let me unlock the front door of a prison I had occasion to visit a couple of times. I want you to take a look around. This prison was actually a couple's home—one of the most beautifully furnished "gulags" I've ever seen. Only one of the two, however, was imprisoned there. The other was the warden.

Here's what I discovered on my first visit. He (the warden) expected her (the unwitting and unwilling prisoner) to show him inordinate "honor and respect." Her unwillingness to display more of these toward him was his justification for demanding she submit to his selfish whims. He wouldn't consider his whims selfish, but I'll let you decide for yourself. He even tried claiming Bible verses that, he said, "authorized" him to make decisions on her behalf. Then he turned to me, expecting support.

"I'm the head of the home, aren't I? If I have to be the fall guy in God's eyes when something goes wrong, I feel it's my right to make decisions that concern us as a couple."

I opened my mouth to say something but never got the chance. The wife moved into his face and fired her words with a vengeance. "That doesn't mean telling me how to cut my hair, what clothes to wear every day, when I must come to bed, or how long I'm required to exercise!"

His selfish demands had lit her fuse. I wanted to speak but couldn't butt into the battle until they had both shot some poorly timed but right-on-target salvos at each other's hearts. In spite of how desperate this couple's words sounded, I felt their verbal exchange was actually a sign of progress. She, the controlled one, was sticking up for herself, and he, the controller, was open to outside counsel.

As they sat on the couch arguing with each other, I caught a glimpse of a framed picture on the table behind them. It was of them on their wedding day. I couldn't help but notice that time had wiped the smiles off their faces and stolen most of the sparkle from their eyes. That's what high control can do to two people who love each other. It can knock the joy out of a relationship in the first few years, then wring out whatever good is left in the partnership over the next 30.

This couple was struggling with a severe case of high control. The young husband was both misguided about his rights and misinformed about what God says regarding leadership in a home.

In the first place, honor and respect cannot be demanded. They're either given or they aren't. If people don't choose to give them, you can't make them. No one has authority, within the confines of a loving home, to compel a person to submit to selfish whims. One of the biggest delusions of this young man was that making personal decisions for his wife, against her will, was part of his God-given position of leadership. They were both leaders, just different kinds. He had been given the responsibility of headship, which simply means "servant-leader." This responsibility did not give him rights over his wife's individual choices.

He tried to foist his personal tastes on his wife, to make her fulfill his mental image of her. He wanted her hair a certain way, he wanted her to wear a certain type of clothes, and he expected her to maintain a certain weight. In a loving relationship, those kinds of issues are individual choices. Healthy love allows for the free exchange of wishes.

A loving husband might say, "I like your hair this way" or "Would you be willing to wear this outfit tonight?" A wife might say, "Would you be willing to wear your hair shorter? I think it makes you look more distin-guished." Healthy love wants to please. Once those wishes or desires are communicated, however, we need to back away from pressuring the other person and let love take over.

Testing the Waters

When Darcy and I first married, I had unrealistic expectations for her. She had her own for me. Early on, we realized we were putting each other in smothering, no-win dilemmas by communicating our expectations without grace. Keep in mind that I'm talking about selfish expectations. For instance, Darcy had certain outfits that I loved for her to wear. A couple of times, I made the mistake of voicing my disappointment in her wardrobe selection just before we walked out the door for the evening. Some of the folly that came from my lips sounded like this:

"Aw nuts, Darcy, I was hoping you were going to wear that cream-colored skirt with the blue blazer." Saying something like that to a woman who has worked for the last 45 minutes to make herself look pretty—and bringing it up two minutes before you're supposed to be leaving—is insane.

Darcy: "Why didn't you mention that before I got dressed?"

Me: "Well, you know I like that outfit. I comment on it every time you wear it."

Darcy: "But Tim, you never *mentioned* it. Besides, this is what I wanted to wear."

Foolish me: "It looks okay (is that a dumb choice of words, or what?), but I would have preferred the skirt and blazer."

By that time, I'd ruined her evening before we were out the door. She was mad I didn't say something earlier. She was mad that I didn't give her, an adult woman, the freedom to wear what she wanted. She became self-conscious about her choice because I was selfish enough to cast doubt over her decision.

I hope this has never happened to you. But early in our marriage, it happened to us more times than I like to admit. These kinds of exchanges still happen when I occasionally slip into the delusion that God has left me in charge of my wife's personal taste.

Nobody would willingly sign a contract binding himself to a life of misery. Nonetheless, some individuals find themselves fighting back tears of disappointment as they assess the nightmare their marriage has become. They look on the marriage certificate as a document that condemns them to a life of suppressing their individuality. Somewhere between driving away from the wedding reception and sitting down to dinner at their first anniversary, a couple's expectations experience a baptism by fire. Let's take romance as a case in point.

Romance isn't always what you thought it would be, is it? Career conflicts, ideas not embraced by a spouse with the enthusiasm you had hoped for, goals renegotiated, disappointing sex—before long, the sharp colors in which you painted your dreams begin to fade. There's enough gloom in that forecast to make many readers look on the institution of marriage as hopeless.

It isn't. It just requires a lot of grace to be maximized and enjoyed. Marriage is the second-hardest relational experience to which an individual ever has to adjust. It requires placing your dreams, disappointments, frailties, and secrets at the mercy of someone who is capable of destroying them and you, and that's risky and tough.

You married with high hopes, however, and you don't want overcontrol to destroy you or your marriage. How do you avoid it? Let's look at three relational dynamics that must be maintained simultaneously in a marriage. They are the crucial levels at which grace-based marriages function.

The Relational Trinity

The First Dynamic: Dependence

One of the main reasons we were attracted to our spouses in the first place was that we had certain needs. Among others, we needed to be needed. The fact that someone would rather be with us, structuring his or her daily schedule around the ability to enjoy our company, is hard for our hearts to pass up.

God designed most of us to need another person in order to feel complete. Peter Blitchington put it this way: "All of God's creation is constructed to avoid self-sufficiency."[1] God placed within us a list of needs that can only be met through being bonded by love to another person. One obvious need is for the sexual expression of our love within the fidelity of the marriage commitment. Some of our needs may seem frivolous, petty, and self-serving—even trite—to outsiders looking in. Perhaps a man needs someone who's a great cook, and a woman needs someone who always checks the locks in the house before he goes to bed. There's nothing wrong with the honest acknowledgment of these needs.

There were a lot of self-serving benefits I hoped to gain when I took Darcy's hand and stepped over the marital threshold. That's because God made me with needs designed to be met through a partnership built on love.

I remember conversations we had during our engagement period. It was then I learned how much she hated to cut grass. She didn't know how to start a lawn mower, and she hoped she would never have to learn as long as she was married to me. I told her how little I knew about cooking, and how I hoped that my aptitude in the culinary arts would actually regress during my marriage to her. The good news was that Darcy loved to cook, and I loved to keep up the lawn.

We discovered, however, that neither of us had much affinity for the vacuum cleaner. We assumed that mutual respect and a desire to meet each other's needs would take care of that. During this "dreaming" stage of our engagement, we felt confident that any problems regarding the vacuum cleaner would fix themselves. But after we dug the rice out of our hair, we realized we both still detested pushing the Electrolux around, and no one was doing it.

We had two options. One was to exercise control over the other person by manipulation, intimidation, power plays, complaining, or whining. The other was to grab the vacuum cleaner and jog a few laps around the family room. Option one was grounded in greed; option two was based on grace. As time went on, our careers were more defined, and time constraints and expediency started to dictate who would do what. We wanted our love to not only survive but flourish, and that required our embracing God's design for our marriage and spurning the world's.

• THE WORLD'S PLAN
  I was at a wedding reception where various toasts were being

proposed for the couple. An uncle of the bride stood up to make his declaration. "Marriage is a 50-50 proposition," he said. "You each do your half and your marriage will endure. May your love enable you to cut the pie equally." Stemware tinkled together throughout the room. A few high-control freaks in the crowd mumbled "Here, here."

My parents taught me enough tact to save some of my dissenting opinions for private conversations, so I said nothing at the time. I had performed the wedding ceremony, however, and felt I had a certain freedom as well as obligation to the couple. The first chance I had to speak to them alone, I gave my perspective on the 50-50 performance relationship.

"You know that toast your uncle gave about marriage being a 50-50 performance relationship?" I said. "Forget it. It won't work."

When they asked why, I told them what I've noticed as well as experienced when it comes to serving another person's needs. The 50-50 performance relationship makes a couple "file keepers." Like it or not, when we feel that each is supposed to be doing half, we unconsciously begin to monitor the other person's contribution to the partnership. Whether the person is holding up his or her half of the deal ultimately becomes irrelevant, because it's impossible to be objective. As an old proverb says, "Each mule assumes his load is the heaviest." The 50-50 performance relationship is an impossibility. It not only doesn't work, but it *can't* work.

Love for a spouse should come from a heart that desires to meet as many of the other's needs as we legitimately can. A simple definition of love may help us see how this can be played out in real time:

> **Love is the commitment of my will,**
> **To your needs and best interests,**
> **regardless of the cost.**[2]

Darcy knows I need to eat but am fairly handicapped when I start rattling pots and pans in the kitchen. It's a need she's eager to meet, even though it takes a lot of effort on her part. Because I love Darcy, I want to do everything I can to meet her dependent needs, too. I know Darcy wants to have enough resources to meet the many expenses that come with raising four children. So I hit the deck each morning and brace my face for the grindstone. Because love is driving me, it seems neither harsh nor unreasonable to expect me to faithfully provide for the financial needs of my family.

• A SEXUAL REVOLUTION

Graciously meeting another's needs demonstrates our love. Leveraging a person's needs against him or her is high control at its most sophisticated level. Some couples' beds have dynamite under them—well, at least that's what it feels like when you see how much one partner uses sex as a weapon. When it comes to sex, high-control relationships generally go to two destructive extremes: demanding and defrauding. Sex is a legitimate, dependent need of each partner. However, each doesn't arrive with the same degree of sexual need. A grace-based relationship doesn't begrudge a partner for having sexual needs and does everything within reason to meet it with sensitivity.

Since sex is a duet, however, it sometimes requires that one person deny the need if the partner is unable—due to illness, stress, discomfort, or fatigue—to pursue or persist. At the same time, in a grace-based relationship, each will do everything possible to be "willing and available" to meet the partner's sexual need.

Mankind's great, great, great grandmother Eve taught her daughters that the greatest power they could exercise over men was in the bedroom. Sex is such an overwhelming need in a man that even the slightest denial of that need by his wife brings his view of himself down a notch. Often, sex is to men what being held is to women—it comforts, reassures, and makes them feel loved. Men "often express themselves sexually when they can't express themselves emotionally."[3] When a wife uses her sexual power to control her husband, it can make him "feel wrong, bad, dirty, embarrassed. It also makes a man feel like he isn't good enough—for if he were a 'real man,' he would be able to make her want him."[4] Further, using a man's sexual drive against him destroys some of the primary adhesive within the marriage.

Paul reminded us that when it comes to sex, we do not have ownership of our bodies—our spouses do. This is the commitment to mutual owner-ship that makes the sexual relationship so strong. He said, *"Stop depriving one another, except by agreement for a time that you may devote yourselves to prayer, and come together again lest Satan tempt you because of your lack of self-control"* (1 Corinthians 7:5).

Depriving a partner of sex is a direct violation of God's mandate to us as married couples. Some spouses (often wives) maintain an attitude of denial of their partners' needs, going so far as to hide behind spirituality and Christian service to legitimize their disobedience to God. Their service to the Lord leaves them "too tired" or "feeling as if sex would be inappropriate at that moment." Ultimately, their denial catches up with them. If you build a house on quicksand, it eventually starts to sink. A husband may emotionally detach from such a wife, go looking elsewhere, separate from her, or even divorce.

God has designed the human body to experience maximum pleasure through sexual climax. High controllers can use even that as a means of control. Sometimes a wife may be satisfied without reaching a climax. That decision should be *hers* to make. But if she is anticipating more fulfillment, a grace-based sexual commitment means her husband will willingly, sensitively, and patiently respond to her need for a climax.

The Second Dynamic: Independence

Some mutually gratifying needs bring us together, but there is also uniqueness within each partner that must remain intact. A healthy marriage leaves plenty of room for a person to maintain independence. Privacy is the first and most obvious way this need is fulfilled.

When Darcy and I were married, we soon realized that it was vital that we respect each other's occasional need to be alone or to work through issues in our own way. In addition, we recognized that, short of wrong priorities, we needed to honor each other's friendships that might not be shared.

Occasionally I meet couples who boast that there's nothing they don't share. They spend all their time together, insist on having mutual friends (or none at all), and never withhold any information from each other, regardless of how painful it might be. They believe that each other's dreams must align and that neither should need anything that can't be fulfilled through or in the presence of the partner.

Usually these couples boast that they have a strong relationship, but they're deluding themselves. The relationship is anything but strong. More often than not, it's an anemic bond, one in which one is overly dependent on the other. Often these relationships are fraught with insecurities, jealousies, and suspicions. These people can't be apart from each other because they don't trust each other. Having observed many of these relationships, I can assure you there is nothing attractive about them.

Shortly after Darcy and I married, I was visiting a couple one afternoon as they worked side by side in their flower garden. It was back when I was still young and inexperienced enough to ask political questions of people I barely knew. A presidential election was a few days away, and I inquired if they had made up their minds about for whom they were going to vote. The man told me his choice. I turned to her and said, "How about you?" She looked at me as though I was missing some obvious principle of life.

"What do you mean, how about me?" she asked.

"I meant whom are *you* planning to vote for?"

She was indignant that I would even consider asking what she thought was obvious. "My husband and I are a team, but he calls the shots," she said. "My submission to him assumes that if he were to make a political decision, I must align with it."

I had read the passages in the New Testament about the relationship between a husband and wife, but I never saw anything that said a wife didn't have the right to her own political views. Obviously and understandably, the views of one partner might influence the other, but healthy love leaves room for individuality and gives each spouse the freedom to make decisions according to his or her own heart.

Not knowing when to quit asking dumb questions, I threw one more at her for clarification. I tried to deliver it with my tongue planted firmly in my cheek. "But when the curtain's pulled, you're in the booth alone, and it's just you and your conscience. Whom do you really want to vote for? What if your husband's political conclusions go against your judgments?"

She looked over at him and picked up his cold stare. "I must submit. It's my duty," she said. That was my signal to bring my questioning to an abrupt end. Her husband had stolen her individuality and buried it deep below the flower bed. It made me sick to see how he worked so hard to give his flowers freedom to bloom but wouldn't let his wife's spirit poke above ground. I realized, by her reply, that neither of them was inviting me to mind their business anymore, so I shut up. But in my heart, I pitied them both. They didn't realize that love doesn't confine individuality—it frees it.

Love gives the other person space—room to breathe, to be unique, to have a dream or two that, though it may not be shared with the same intensity, still needs to be encouraged. All of what I've said, of course, assumes that no one's dependent or independent needs violate any clearly stated biblical guideline.

The Third Dynamic: Interdependence

A grace-based marriage recognizes both the personal, dependent needs and the individual, independent needs and wraps them all up in an *interdependent* package. The word contains its own definition. It means we work together to bring out the best in each other by allowing dependence and independence to coexist in the relationship. Love constrains us to do everything we can to meet a partner's dependent needs without punishing him for having them. Love doesn't tell a partner how she must make personal choices. At the same time, it doesn't assume responsibility for someone else's choices. Rather, it concentrates on what it can give to a relationship regardless of what it gets in return, and regardless of personal price or inconvenience.

It's for precisely this reason that so many couples struggle. They let their selfish wants and fragile fears take over and, as a result, coerce a certain behavior or attitude from the spouse. This is self-destructive love. Grace-based love doesn't shame a spouse for having needs or begrudge him a reasonable amount of independence, and it recognizes that when dependence and independence move in harmony, a couple is interdependent on each other for the pursuit of joy.

Amazing Grace

If a couple wants to maintain a grace-based relationship, a pleasing template in the Word of God gives them an easy checklist to follow. It was written by a man who learned about grace-based relationships by traveling the back roads of Palestine during the Lord's three-year public ministry. He learned some of his lessons the hard way, and he never forgot them.

Let's look at what Jesus' disciple, Simon Peter, had to say about relationships grounded in grace:

*To sum up, let all be harmonious, sympathetic, brotherly,
kindhearted, and humble in spirit; not returning evil for evil, or
insult for insult, but giving a blessing instead; for you were called
for the very purpose that you might inherit a blessing. For, "let
him who means to love life and see good days refrain his tongue
from evil and his lips from speaking guile. And let him turn away
from evil and do good; let him seek peace and pursue it. For the eyes
of the Lord are upon the righteous, and His ears attend to their
prayer, but the face of the Lord is against those who do evil."*

1 Peter 3:8-12

This passage gives us guidelines for performing two crucial commitments within marriage. First, it shows us how to respond to one another through grace. Second, it shows us what to do if we've been harming our partners by selfishly controlling them.

A Checklist for Grace-Based Love

1. Live harmoniously

I played in the orchestra in both high school and college. Before a concert, we'd take our seats on the stage and begin warming up. Since I was a brass player, I'd warm up my lip by playing exercises. Everyone warmed up in his own way. Because we were all doing our own thing, anyone listening might find his ears hurting from the discord. Ultimately the first chair clarinetist would stand up and play a sustained concert B flat. That was the signal for all of us to stop what we were doing and start tuning up to that note. Brass players would adjust slides, woodwinds would make their instruments longer or shorter, and the string section would tighten or loosen the pegs of their instruments. When the last instrument went silent, the conductor would enter from the side, raise his baton, and we would play harmoniously.

Christ is to be the concert B flat of our marriage relationships. His presence in our marriages frees the Holy Spirit to make beautiful music through us to God's glory.

2. Live sympathetically

In the verse just before the passage listed above, Peter told husbands how God expects them to treat their wives: *"You husbands likewise, live with your wives in an understanding way, as with a weaker vessel, since she is a woman; and grant her honor as a fellow heir of the grace of life, so that your prayers may not be hindered"* (1 Peter 3:7).

God makes it as clear as our bicep muscles that we men are to deal with our wives as delicate and priceless vessels. That's what that word *weaker* is all about. We're to honor them by never using our physical strength, which is usually greater than theirs, against them, and we are never to dishonor their intuitive skills, which give them a strong capacity to emote. We're to see them as equals—co-heirs of the grace of life.

Men, you need to know that God doesn't pull any punches about how He'll deal with us if we don't treat our wives properly. He says He'll hinder our prayers. Our access to Him will be either limited or denied depending on how disobedient we are to His commands. He has given us our wives as gifts. Abusing them with our overbearing power says something to Him about what we think of His gift.

But lest wives think this passage is directed only at their husbands, it helps to take a closer look. Hidden just below the surface is a nugget of truth for the woman who wants to love by grace. It says that the woman is the "weaker" vessel, right? So that must make the husband the "weak" vessel. The point of the passage is not that the husband is strong and the wife is weak, but that they're *both* weak. One's just more delicate than the other.

Women need to understand that they can kill the spirit of a husband through the methods of control they use: passive control, aggressive control, or a poisonous combination of both. Peter asked wives to consider the stewardship God has placed in their hands and deal with their husbands in an understanding way. Think of it like this: A wife is a delicate vase; a husband is a crock. Both are breakable, but one is much stronger than the other. Throw a crock to the floor hard enough, however, and it, too, will smash.

When we're sympathetic with each other, we maintain an affinity for each other that drives us to try to understand how our mates are receiving the treatment we give. When we're sympathetic to their needs, living harmoniously is a lot easier.

3. Be committed to each other like brothers.

A brother will always be there when you need him. Obviously, in some unfortunate families, that statement is more idealistic than realistic. But in most families it's true. Grace-based marriages have priorities where partners assure each other that they'll always be there...

...in the good days as well as the bad.

...when they have plenty and when they don't have a dime,

...when they're healthy and when the body, emotions, or spirit are having a tough time,

...whether it costs little or much,

...until one of them lays the other into the arms of God.

4. Show kindness

God tells us to maintain a disposition that is helpful, gentle, and eager to meet our partner's needs. High control stabs this mandate in the heart. Because high control is driven by incorrect assumptions about the authority or responsibility we have in another person's life, it doesn't approach the other with a heart of kindness.

5. Be humble

God wants us to put our partners' best interests above our own. A good way to do this is by taking a subordinate position that shows we're eager to help and happy to please. Couples who treat each other this way find themselves drawn closer to each other in love. As a result, their mutual desire to be the kind of person the partner needs grows within them until it ultimately shows up in changed behavior.

Harmony, sympathy, brotherly kindness, and humility—these characteristics sound fine on paper. But what happens when they're not a reality? Peter anticipated this reality and gave some solid advice: *"Not returning. . . insult for insult, but giving a blessing instead"* (1 Peter 3:9).

As we read down Peter's list, we're tempted to think, *That's easy for you to say, St. Peter, but suppose my partner is a selfish egotist who's smothering me with his high-controlling ways?* Peter anticipated that problem. He said, "Don't exchange verbal salvos with him, but give him a blessing instead."

The best way to give a blessing is to *be* a blessing. Don't do what's sinful. Do what's in the best interest of your partner. Peter said that when you do, you will inherit a blessing. It's a sacrifice with a promise attached. An inheritance is normally understood as a gift that's waiting for us somewhere down the road. We may not receive it until we some day stand before God, but He won't forget. We *will* receive it.

Dealing with Your High-Control Tendencies

For those whose hearts ache over the pain they've administered to their partners through the high control they've maintained over them, Peter gave some advice:

Stop It.
Fix It.

Peter said that if we want to enjoy life and have a decent future, we must stop mishandling our position in marriage. For starters, we can stop using our tongues to communicate evil. High control is evil. Peter pleaded with us to stop it! He further warned that our lips should refrain from speaking guile. What's guile? It means to trick our partners. In other words, we're not to mislead or overpower our spouses through cunning or cleverness. That's one of the many ways that high control can demonstrate itself.

Peter then moved from our words to our actions and repeated his rebuke to those whose control is more than verbal. "Stop it," he said. "Do good, and make your life a commitment to being all your partner needs, even if there's nothing in it for you."

The last part of his advice has to do with our responsibility toward the person we've been unfairly controlling. "Fix it," he said. This implies taking responsibility for our actions. Peter urged us to "seek peace." That means we're to confess our sin to our partners, assume responsibility for the negative consequences, and then be reconciled to each other. That's where "pursuing" comes in. It means that we, the controllers, should keep working to make peace for the damage we've done. And should that peace occur, we must maintain it by refusing to control anymore.

Nothing in Peter's instruction indicates that it was given as mutual counsel. It's individual. In other words, we should make a unilateral commitment to following Peter's instructions regardless of our partners' attitudes or actions. Therefore, whether we're the controller or the controlled, we're to love our mates with grace-based love and do everything we can to rectify the wrongs we've done.

"You Need a Friend"

It was the calm after the storm. Darcy and I had finally wrestled and cajoled our four children into dreamland. We had been hip deep in bathwater, Ninja Turtle pajamas, Super Mario Brothers toothpaste, teddy bears, Go-bots, and cinnamon-flavored dental floss. Stories had been told, prayers had been whispered, and lullabies had been hummed. The respite hit me at once as I sat down in front of the fire to enjoy some quiet reflection.

Even when we're both tired, Darcy knows how to make the most of moments. She had mentioned earlier that she wanted to teach me how to work with our daughters' hair so that on those occasions when I didn't have her skills to rely on, I could still send the girls out the door looking halfway decent. That's what gave her the idea of using this quiet time to teach me how to French braid hair.

Don't laugh. Someone has to do it. Of our four children, two are daughters. And it had become apparent to Darcy that in spite of my best intentions, I fell dismally short when it came to grooming the girls' hair. Until they were old enough to do their own, I needed to be prepared to help. Both Karis and Shiloh have long, beautiful hair. On the occasions when I had tried to get it to conform to some sort of aesthetic standard, I'd failed miserably.

This explained the brush and rubber bands in Darcy's hands as she tuned in an "easy listening" station on the stereo. I sat on the couch while she sat on the floor, staring at the fire, with her back toward me. Her long, brunette hair was to be my laboratory. So with a rubber band in my teeth, a brush in one hand, and more hair than I knew what to do with in the other, I proceeded to divide the strands of her hair into three equal clumps and start the weave that gives the French braid its famous look.

When you're a clumsy guy with no aptitude for women's hairstyles, nothing good is going to happen on the first attempt—or on the second, third, or fourth. I kept weaving it down, shaking my head at the mess, brushing it out, and starting again. Over and over. The first time I actually completed a weave (rubber band and everything), I mentioned to Darcy that she might not want to wear it out in public. Then I pulled out the band, brushed, and started weaving again.

Every once in a while, you notice something that's been right in front of you all your life but gone undetected. I've seen thousands of girls' braids in my four decades. And this certainly wasn't the first time I'd seen how a braid is made. But it was the first time I made this particular observation: I was weaving three separate strands of hair into the overlapping pattern that formed the braid, but when the braid was completed, it looked as if it were made of just two strands. I thought how this observation should be classified as one of the great mysteries of life: Two are really three, and without the third, the two are not at all.

I love James Taylor's music. He's one of the baby boomer's favorite pastimes. While I was braiding and observing this mystery about two being three and three making two, JT's classic tune "You've Got a Friend" started coming from the stereo. I sang along with him.

> *You just call out my name, and you know wherever I am,*
> *I'll come running to see you again....*
> *Winter, spring, summer, or fall,*
> *All you've got to do is call.*
> *And I'll be there, yes I will,*
> *You've got a friend.*[5]

Darcy and I have a mutual Friend. He has woven His life so much into the fabric of our life together that even though, from the outside in, we may appear to be two people, in reality we're three. And because He's in our lives, He enables our love to fall into a much-more-beautiful pattern.

Grace-based marriages don't simply happen. They're the result of careful decisions and divine commitments. Those who want to free themselves from the tyranny of high control need to weave Jesus into their partnership. Just the touch of His grace can overwhelm and overcome. The three appear to be two, and the two become one.

I bent over and breathed a kiss on the top of Darcy's braided hair. We, indeed, have a Friend.

CHAPTER 14

Grace-Based Parenting

When my parents first introduced me to their friends Ike and
Becky, I sensed something was seriously wrong in their home.
Although I was a lot younger than their kids, and Ike and Becky
were a lot older than my parents, in my untutored mind, I still felt that the
way they dealt with their kids was going to end up causing a lot of hardship.

I was five or six when I first made their acquaintance at church. Because
they were part of my parents' large circle of friends, I didn't feel threatened
in spite of what I detected as an inherent flaw in their family. Don't
misunderstand me. I wasn't some little "shrink" running around church,
scrutinizing everyone's shortcomings. It's just that Ike and Becky seemed
more bent on controlling each other than any other couple I knew. And
they weren't above using their kids as weapons in the process. They stood in
such stark contrast to my parents and others I knew.

I was one of six kids, and my folks had received little training for the
parenting challenge they took on. In spite of their limited backgrounds,
however, they seemed to parent their kids from a foundation of truth and a
lot of common sense. All in all, I'd say they did a good job. And more than
anything else, their treatment of me was what made me pity Ike and Becky's
kids—especially their boys.

A digression would help here. In contrast to my father, who came from more humble means, Ike had been brought up in a privileged environment. He was one of two sons, but because of his father's high standing in the community, as well as the gap in age between him and his brother, Ike had been raised like an only child. Becky came from good stock, too. She had been introduced to Ike by his parents, so their marriage was all but arranged.

The problems in their family came after the birth of their twin sons. Becky had a tough time delivering them, and when that happens, it sometimes affects the way a mother bonds to a child. In this case, she attached more to one than to the other.

I remember the boys well. They weren't identical twins like those I'd seen in school. In fact, they were about as opposite as two boys could be. One was extremely aggressive, very masculine, and constantly venturing out into the world around him. He was also the one who seemed to get into trouble the most. His twin brother didn't look anything like him. He didn't think anything like him, either. He was more of a mama's boy, which made it a lot easier for her to manage him. For those reasons, plus a host of others, she let her heart gravitate closer to him until it was obvious to all us outsiders that he was her favorite. His brother knew it, too.

Maybe that's what caused Ike to compensate the way he did. Realizing the brothers were being torn apart by his wife's favoritism, he over-attached to the other boy in a way that could only be construed as favoritism, too. With each boy being a parent's pet, it was only logical that a lot of emotional turmoil would follow.

I watched their family being torn apart by the ways the parents played one boy against the other. Ike, like a lot of men, wasn't the most sensitive husband. He was so preoccupied with the business empire he was building that he failed to give Becky the attention a strong marriage requires. All this caused Becky to dote more on her favorite son and use him like a pawn in power plays against Ike.

Everybody in the church knew this was going on, but no one could do anything about it. However, a few people observed the nightmare in this home and took serious notice for their own families. That was probably the only good thing that came out of all this. We were all observing what happens when parents exercise illegitimate control over their kids.

Of the two parents, Becky was the most manipulative. It was interesting to see how quickly her "favorite" picked up her ways. Whatever my contact with him in the years since I first met him, I've never felt I could trust him. He was tutored in deceit by his manipulative mother, and his track record indicates she taught him well.

His brother hasn't fared that well either, come to think of it. He struggles with his identity and has felt a sense of homelessness in his spirit. He is almost like a man without a country, and all because his parents thought their selfish needs could and should take precedence over the building of righteous character in their children.

Everything came to a head shortly before Ike died. Rather than wait until he was dead and have his will transfer his estate to his children, he decided to divide it up in advance. Becky was certain he wasn't going to slice it down the middle, and this was unacceptable to her. Ike didn't care. Becky didn't feel she had any legal recourse for changing his mind. That's what drove her to take advantage of the leverage she had carried in her favorite son's heart. She played him like a cello, telling him just what to do, and in the end he tricked his elderly father into reapportioning the estate to his own advantage.

His brother went ballistic when he realized what had happened, but it was too late to do anything about it. In his desperation, he tried to get his father to fix the mess his brother and mother had conspired to make, but the legal red tape surrounding the exchange of assets made it impossible. That's when their family feud began, and it continues to this day.

By now you've probably figured out who those boys were. You, like me, met them in church—in Sunday school, to be exact. The boys' names: Jacob and Esau. Their hatred has been legendary for several thousand years now, all because of two manipulative parents who wanted their own way too much.

Power-Broker Parents

Clearly, the area where we struggle the most with the issue of control is in our role as parents. We have authority and responsibility before God to steward carefully the children He has given us, and in our zeal to fulfill our role well, we sometimes step over the line. Add to that the sheer complexities that come with the job. Children drain more emotional energy from our hearts than just about any other pressure we face. Their maintenance alone is more than a plateful. But add to that all the complex moral, emotional, spiritual, and volitional frustrations we must help them contend with, and we can easily find ourselves approaching overload. Exercising undo control over them is the easy way out of this situation—and many parents turn to it daily.

Besides the stewardship and the difficulty of the job, other factors that move parents into controlling their kids can leave lifelong hurts in their children's hearts. Sometimes it's the fact that the parents came from an unfortunate home. They were short-changed by their own parents in the area of emotional confidence, so they gravitate to overcontrol to compensate for their dilemma. Sometimes parents are salving deep disappointments from their present situation: divorce, abandonment, illness, unemployment, debt, or a host of other pressures. Maybe it's fear, rage, or shame that has them in bondage. Any of these, as we've learned, can create a high-control parent. And for some people, of course, control just comes naturally, without any pressure exerted from other areas.

Regardless of the reason, parents are the most notorious controllers on the globe, and because of their privileged position, they do more to propagate the problem than any other group. Many children, if they were asked to come up with a synonym for the word *parent*, would say "power." It has always been a power position. But nothing in God's Word ever gave a parent the right to be a power broker.

Let me tell you about Cindy. She had heard I was working on this book and thought her story might shed some light, so she sent me a tape. As I listened to her voice and heard the incidents from her life, I couldn't help but think that she was an example of what any parent could produce if we simply let our wills go unbridled.

Cindy said her adult years have been preoccupied with trying to define who she is. Her mother's crimes against her heart had left her but a shell. I hope she will ultimately get to fill that shell with someone she can feel is significant. Listen to her words:

"I guess when you factor everything down to its lowest common denominator, Mom didn't know how to love us. But she had to raise us. So she did the only other thing within her grasp—she controlled us. It was the easy way out for her. She was smarter, bigger, and more powerful than all us kids put together. She was also miserable, which drove her to use all her advantages against us. Dad turned from a husband to a drunk shortly after I was born. He turned from a drunk to an occasional visitor after my sister was born. And after my brother was born, he turned invisible.

"I'm not sure which feeling overwhelmed me the most while I was growing up, the feeling that I was a prisoner or the feeling that I was a slave. Probably they're just variations of the same nightmare. Mom made us do the housework. That's a normal responsibility for children, but loving parents always think about the size and capabilities of the child. Mom didn't. She expected us to do the work as thoroughly and as quickly as she could. We were just kids.

"When I was real young, we lived in a large, older house. One of the jobs she gave me was dusting the eight-inch baseboards throughout the house. It would take me a good part of Saturday morning. She'd inspect it. If she found places where I didn't do a good enough job, instead of having me fix that part, she'd make me do the whole thing over.

"I give her credit for wanting to instill a good work ethic in us. The problem was that she often accompanied our failures at working with physical and verbal abuse. If we made a mistake, we heard about it for a long, long time afterward. She would exile me to my room and then stand at the foot of my bed, telling me what a disappointment I was to her. She was relentless about it. She'd make the point, then drive it through my heart until I ran out of tears to shed. I'd cry so much it would leave me with a headache. But she never came to me to let me know that things would be okay.

"In fact, I never remember her telling me she loved me. She never hugged me. In all our family photos, there are no pictures of Mom with her arms around any of us. I think it was one of her many ways of controlling us. She knew how much we longed for it.

"She didn't allow us any privacy, either. She went so far as removing the doorknobs from our bedroom doors. She did this after we locked her out of our room during one of her tirades. Taking the locks off our doors was another way of dominating us, and it was very effective.

"We weren't allowed to be creative. If she wanted something done, we had to do it her way. Even if it was something for ourselves, like doing a homework assignment, she insisted we do it her way. As an adult, it's still difficult for me to be creative, because I never got the freedom to develop that dimension of my life.

"Another way she controlled us was through shame. She had a way of humiliating me that left me feeling totally exposed. One event stands out in my mind. It seared my soul so much that it seems as though it's suspended in time—an omnipresent sense of my own inadequacy. I was past the age when it's supposed to happen, but I wet my pants. I was about four or five years old. She was so angry at me that she put a diaper on me and made me sit on the front porch in broad daylight. I begged her to not make me do it—someone would see me. She didn't back down. Sure enough, my girlfriend came by, came up on the porch, and saw me.

"Mom put a lot of emphasis on our looks. In fact, she was obsessed with them. I realize now that it was one more way she used us to control the outside world. Even though everything was out of control within the walls of our house, she could make it appear otherwise to outsiders by dressing us up on Christmas, Easter, or for school so that we looked perfect. It was all part of the facade we had to maintain to cover for the unacceptable ways she controlled us.

"Of all the ways my mother controlled us, the worst thing she did was to abandon us. She would turn her back on us when we failed, withdraw from us if she was in one of her moods, and even threaten to leave us. I have a lot of painful memories haunting my soul, but without doubt my worst one is this withdrawal.

"I was eight years old. My sister was three. We slept together. My father had fallen into the pattern of working late and then going straight to the bars. Mom finally had enough of his behavior. My sister and I had been asleep for some time. It was very late. Mother woke us both out of a deep sleep and made us come downstairs and sit on the bottom step. She told us she was leaving. 'If Daddy doesn't feel he needs to be here, then neither do I.' She just stood there telling us she was leaving us. I remember I was crying and my sister was screaming. She made us sit there on that step while she walked out the door.

"I can't remember anything that happened after that. But I have that snapshot of her abandoning us that night. After that, we did everything she demanded of us for fear she'd leave us alone again.

"I'm learning a lot about forgiveness as a result of all this. It hasn't happened for me yet. I'm convinced forgiveness is a process anyway. The Holy Spirit has softened my heart toward the pain of my past. Through His help, I've been able to let go of a lot of anger, hurt, and resentment that was handed down to me as my birthright. Perhaps someday I'll understand Mom a little better, and maybe then I'll be able to offer the gift I know I need to give her if I ever want to love her freely—the gift of forgiveness. For now, I'm just trying to cope the best I can."

When I shut off the tape recorder, I bowed my head and prayed for this young woman with a broken heart. She was the victim of a parental power struggle that will haunt her for a long time. But she's working through some steps that will free her enough to be able to alter her birthright and give her future children a legacy of love.

Obviously, Cindy's mom was an extreme case of control. I'll take it a step further: She was sick. Her control was clearly in the realm of child abuse. But she illustrates what can be found even in nice Christian homes, albeit to a much lesser degree. Although we may not be sick like Cindy's mom, our controlling tendencies, regardless how minor, can still undermine the grace God has called us to build into our children's lives.

How often do we insist children do things *our way* simply because it's easier than letting them figure things out through creative experimentation? How often do we give them jobs beyond their capabilities and then get frustrated when they can't perform up to the standards of people much older? How often do we insist on controlling the image our children portray to the world so we can manipulate, through them, the way people view us?

Karis was in the first grade. A conflict was boiling in her bedroom, a power struggle between two extremely capable wills—hers and her mother's. Darcy had picked out her school outfit, and Karis was balking, holding up her own choice. Throughout Karis's kindergarten year, Darcy had selected 99 percent of her outfits. Darcy had two primary reasons for doing that: She had an excellent eye for what looked good, and Karis didn't. How could she? She was only seven years old.

"What's wrong?" I asked from the hallway.

"Karis wants to wear this outfit. It doesn't do anything for her. She's resisting over what I want her to wear."

As a man with little or no taste in first-grade-girls' clothing, I couldn't discern the advantages of one outfit over another. As a person who has to write a lot of checks every year to put "outfits" in my kids' closets, I was trying to determine why Darcy ever bought Karis an outfit that "doesn't do anything for her."

Karis took the outfit Darcy had picked out, laid it on her bed, and proceeded to shed her nightgown and comply with her mother's wishes. Darcy was happy, and I was relieved that we got out of the incident so easily. Obedience often gives you that illusion. But it was obvious that Darcy and I needed to talk about the dilemma we were in. This was just round one of what would be many battles over the choices Karis wanted to make.

The discussion went like this:

"You know, Darcy, that conflict is going to occur more frequently as she gets older."

"I know. So what are you thinking?"

"I think we're stuck in a trap, and we'd prefer to take the easy way out."

"You mean she wants to grow up, but we don't want to take the risks that accompany mistakes she'll make trying to figure everything out for herself?"

"That's precisely the problem. She wants independence and freedom to make some choices for herself. She needs it, too, in order to feel complete and significant. But her taste in clothes—it's unbelievable sometimes."

"And it reflects on me when she goes waltzing into school dressed like some serial killer."

"It's not that bad, Darc. It just *seems* that way. When we cut through all of this, though, the fact remains that our job is to get her to the point where she can make wise choices—clothing is just one of them. And even though she doesn't meet the standards you or I desire, we still need to let her experiment."

Darcy and I wanted to control an area in Karis's life that doesn't fall in some moral, black-and-white category. As she was getting older, we were discovering that there were lots of areas like that. We weren't doing her any good telling her, or even mildly hinting to her, the way we'd like her to decide in all these personal situations. Certainly not if we wanted her to learn through trial and error. It especially wasn't right when one of our primary motives was to make things easier on ourselves.

Obviously there are areas—like morals, safety, and preparation for adulthood—where parents must call the shots. But there are far more areas in children's lives that don't fall into these life-or-death, do-or-die categories, and these are the very areas where well-meaning but misguided parents can violate their children's spirits. In the process, we rob them of the grace they need to grow up confidently.

Our "crisis in the closet" was ultimately decided through compromise. For first grade, Darcy would pick out three outfits a week, Karis two. In second grade, the ratio would flip-flop. In third grade, it would be Darcy one, Karis four. After that, it was all up to Karis. Of course guidelines were set. She had to dress modestly, she had to dress for the season (we live in Phoenix, and wool in May is murder), and she had to comply with the school schedule (tennis shoes on PE day, party apparel for festivities, etc.). Within those guidelines, she was off and running. By third grade, she was choosing well enough that Darcy felt comfortable in handing the whole area of clothing selection over to her.

A few times along the way, she walked into the kitchen in clothing combinations that caused Darcy and I to look at each other and shake our heads. We knew the teachers at school probably wondered about the parents behind such a child. But we can't let how others perceive us or our children cause us to control our kids in areas where they can (or should) be making their own choices. If we didn't want people to think badly about us, we would never have had kids in the first place.

The process of preparing children for responsible adulthood assumes that some of their learning experiences will blow up in our faces while our friends look on. Kids are adults in the making. They can't make sound choices every time. But they can get to where they're fairly reliable. That's why it's essential that we give them plenty of practice with the day-to-day choices, especially the ones that have minimal negative consequences.

Control or Under Control?

Back in the second chapter, I said that the Bible teaches we're not supposed to control other people. There's this thin line, this boundary, between what is our responsibility and what belongs to them. Control happens when we slip past that boundary and assume authority over someone else in an area where we have no such right.

In the story above, Darcy and I were trying to assume responsibility for how Karis appeared to others, as well as how she made us appear. Part of our desire was for Karis's best interests. But part of it was clearly for our own selfish interests. And continuing to make choices for her would have helped us at her expense—and *that*, when you distill it to its basic components, is control. Whether we were doing it for her or for us, it was better for Karis that we gradually hand those choices over to her. They would ultimately give her more responsibility for herself—something for which the human spirit longs.

When we try to protect children from failure by making decisions for them, we not only discourage them, but we handicap them, too. They don't feel like true participants in the activities that make up their lives. Furthermore, they develop a sense of being victims. Then they can develop a mind-set that they aren't really to blame when they make mistakes, which leads them to not assume responsibility for their actions.

I also mentioned earlier that every time we see someone in the Bible slip over the thin line of responsibility and exercise control, it turned out badly. The actions were resented and, eventually, the controllers were resented as well. We further observed that Jesus Christ, the God-man who had the genuine right and power to control people, never exercised His option. He left the choices to us. But He also left us with the total responsibility for those choices.

I assume a question has crossed your mind as you weigh all this against the backdrop of your role as a parent. *I thought the Bible teaches that we parents, are* **supposed** *to control our children. Doesn't it?*

Does it?

The clearest passage on the subject is 1 Timothy 3:4-5. Paul wrote a letter to his understudy Timothy, instructing him on the management and government of the local church. In this particular passage, he outlined the qualifications for the overseers, or elders, of the church. He said,

> *He must be one who manages his own household well, keeping his children* **under** *control with all dignity (but if a man does not*

know how to manage his own household, how will he take care of the church of God?) (emphasis added)

An elder is to keep his children *under* control—not control them. We're discussing the difference between night and day when we compare "control" with "under control." Keeping children under control assumes boundaries, values, moral absolutes, expectations, consequences, and discipline. It means we are providing the kind of leadership and direction that helps them exercise their spiritual options and maximize their individual potential.

Control, as defined above, disregards the children's need for independence, uniqueness, and individuality. While parents may have the kids' best interests in mind, they are also making choices that make *them* feel more confident and happy. They're placing too much emphasis on their own best interests.

As we've seen, some of the most dangerous controllers in the family can clothe their agendas in ways that seem to be genuinely in the best interests of the person being controlled. When children are being controlled by a parent, however, they become confused. They know there's something selfish about the pressure they're getting from Mom or Dad, but because the parents hold the position of authority in their lives, they feel they have no recourse.

Rebellion during children's teenage years is often little more than an attempt to gain enough breathing space from their parents to figure out who they are—and what their relationship with God is going to be.

Preparing children for independence is not only our job, but it's also the best way we can help them develop their faith. If God doesn't force Himself on us, should we force ourselves and Him on our kids? Don't misunderstand. Parents have a clear responsibility to make certain choices, set clear boundaries, administer discipline, maintain certain moral and quality standards, and intervene at times when children need to make "mid-course corrections." But these are all to be done in the grace-based environment God has asked us to create in order to bring His children to maturity.

Obviously, the younger our children are, the more involved we need to be in their day-to-day choices. As I developed in my book *Raising Kids Who Turn Out Right*,[1] the younger years are the time when we are called to *protect* them. But as they get older, we're supposed to shift more from protector to mentor (one who prepares them). It's not that they move into an unprotected sphere; it's just that they're now protected by the skills we've given them. Life on their own (or with a partner) should never catch them unaware. They should have had enough practice in independence to have most of the kinks worked out by the time they leave us to make their own way in life.

High-control parents withhold empowerment from their children. They're not willing to risk what their children's inadequacies might cost them in time, energy, or social status, so they manipulate them. Sadly, however, when these children grow into adults, their inadequacies end up dominating them. I have dealt with many people in their twenties and thirties who feel inept in their careers and vital relationships because their parents were afraid to let them make choices as children.

Many of the overcontrolling parents of baby boomers have been shocked in their twilight years to discover what their tendencies did to their children. They expected to enjoy their last semester of life doing more-leisurely things, kicking back, relaxing. Instead, they're still working to pay expenses for grown kids who are still living off them. Their baby boomers became baby boomerangers. Controlling their children rather than keeping them under control created emotionally and vocationally anemic adults. Now guilt continues to drive these parents.

The following chart illustrates how the responsibility for choices is to shift over to our children as we raise them from birth to maturity.

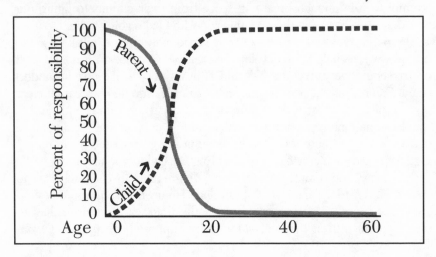

Notice how the level of responsibility shifts as children get older. Building conscientious children requires that we transfer responsibility to them from early in their childhood. The older they get, the less we keep and the more they assume. By the time they hit their early teens, they should be making the majority of their daily choices. In the last year or two before they ship out for their adult adventure, we should give over the last few areas of responsibility.

When they finally go, they are totally responsible for their own lives. We move from a resource to a reference point. If we've been developing them accordingly, adulthood won't be a hardship. In fact, our careful transferring of responsibility to them makes the transition into adulthood so smooth that we and they barely notice the difference.

The key to this process is that we don't intervene in the consequences of our children's choices. When our oldest was in third grade, she fell into a pattern of getting ready for school that left her running for the bus almost daily. This pushed Darcy into a role of hounding and hurrying her to get her out the door and to the bus stop on time. It helps to understand that the bus stop is a few hundred feet from our house. Each morning she was letting more and more things distract her. We warned her that if she didn't make the bus, she was going to have to walk to school. I had called her principal to find out what the consequences were for tardiness.

"First time," he said, "she just gets a mark for being tardy. Second time, she gets a mark and has to come to my office. I yell at her for a few minutes about being late. The third time, it's counted as an absence against her record, it could affect her conduct grade, she has to serve a detention after school, and you or Darcy have to bring her in the next day to check her back in."

"Perfect," I said.

She called our bluff.

The bus went chugging by our house one morning shortly thereafter, and she hadn't even started eating the breakfast that had been sitting in front of her for 15 minutes.

"Okay, Honey, let's go," I said.

"Are you going to take me to school?"

"Kind of."

She got her stuff and herself into my car. (Her school was too far away to let her walk all the way alone.) I drove her to the street her school was on, coming to a stop at a corner about three-tenths of a mile away. From that vantage point, I could watch her all the way to the school.

"This is all the farther the taxi goes today, Babe," I said.

"But Daddy, I'm late."

"I know, but you got up at 6:30 this morning and had plenty of time to be ready. You made the choices that set all of these consequences in motion. Now you have to bear them."

"But, Daddy, I'm *so* late."

"If you want to sit here and debate all this, it's your choice, but it's going to make you that much later. This is all the farther this car and this dad are taking you."

She grabbed her things and jumped out the door. Saddle oxfords, lunch box, book bag, and blonde hair danced as she ran. But before she got a hundred feet, she raced back to my side of the car, stuck her face inside, and kissed me good-bye. I watched her head bob up and down as she ran all the way to school.

The opposite of controlling children, therefore, is handing over legitimate responsibility to them. But knowing when to relinquish certain options and choices is tricky. Let me suggest a few questions you can ask yourself in any given situation:

1. Can the child make this decision himself?
2. If he can't, should he be capable of making it by now?
3. What, short of my own self-interest, is keeping him from making this decision?
4. If he makes this decision and it isn't what I want, am I willing to:
   a. accept it?
   b. let him face whatever consequences (good or bad) go with his choice?

As emotionally draining as it may be, keeping kids under control rather than controlling them actually "nets" a more bearable parenting style. You may have to walk through the valley of the shadow of adolescence with them and feel utterly alone in the process. But transferring responsibility to them is the grace-based way to go. It's also the way to help them move into adulthood with confidence.

More Help Than They Need

The area where many conscientious moms and dads fall into over-control is the spiritual realm. Parents want their children to have a strong relationship with the Lord and to make a series of choices reflecting their commitment to Him. If they don't make those choices, parents may be tempted to administer undue influence to try to make it happen. Parents make them:

- go to every youth meeting,
- hang around only with the friends *they* find spiritually acceptable,
- serve in various ministry capacities,
- accept *their* version of God's will for their lives.

But the results of such forced spirituality might not be genuine. Indeed, most times they're not. Jamming Christianity into a child's heart normally backfires. "If we have a tendency to control, one of the most dangerous traps we can fall into is feeling that we know God's will for another person. Control, then, puts on a spiritual mask and is much harder to recognize—and to escape."[2]

We can encourage, model, and lead our children down the path to spiritual maturity. But a relationship with God can't be coerced if we want it to be genuine. We can't make children be anything on the inside—only on the outside. We do much better to create a loving, noncoercive environment and leave to the Lord the responsibility of drawing our children's hearts to Himself. If we prod our children into following our spiritual agenda for them, we are taking God's place. We need to let God do what He's going to do, and in His time frame. Paul said, *"I planted, Apollos watered, but God was causing the growth"* (1 Corinthians 3:6). God is the only one truly capable of bringing about spiritual maturity. To intervene in His role is to circumvent His best for our children.

Besides the spiritual life, there's a mile-long list of other areas where parents are inclined to make choices for their children. These, too, are easy for us to justify as well-meaning. Choosing their hobbies, academic paths, obsessions, careers, mates, and so on can sound like legitimate intervention. But in the end, we've made choices with which *they* must live. If a choice we make doesn't set well with them (which happens often), they'll end up resenting it—and us, for making it for them. Grace-based parenting is supposed to empower. Personal ownership of life's choices is essential to having a heart that lives with a sense of freedom.

Stepping Way Over the Bounds

Some forms of parental control can never be justified. These actions may be selfish, arrogant, mean-spirited, vicious, and evil. Cindy, whom I mentioned earlier in this chapter, had a mom who was disappointed over a lot of things and used her children as whipping posts for her anger. Four things need to be said about parents who exercise evil control over their children:
1. They will live to regret it.
2. They are creating generational damage.
3. They need to stop it.
4. And they need to seek reconciliation with their children and with God for their actions.

They may need to seek help in pulling this off. That's what pastors and competent Christian counselors are for. Courageously gaining the benefit of these skilled helpers could heal a lot of broken hearts and save a lot of broken homes.

Empowering Your Children

As I said earlier, controlling our children deflates them, while granting them the privileges of responsibility builds their self-confidence. I'd like to close this chapter with a checklist for empowering our children's spirits.

1. Give them ownership of as many assets as you can as soon as you can.
Kids need to be taught stewardship and the careful management of assets. What assets can you provide?
• RELATIONAL ASSETS: Give them access to your network of friends, and give them choices in the selection of their own network. Obviously, you may have to intervene if someone within their network poses a clear threat to their safety. But while you're intervening, you may want to study what is (or was) going on within your family that might have pushed them to choose the wrong kind of friends.

• MATERIAL ASSETS: Create outlets for them to make money. Among other things, you might give them an allowance for consistently displaying responsibility toward household chores. Part-time jobs, of course, can help, too. But you've got to be careful that one responsibility doesn't destroy another. Jobs that take our children out of their church youth group, especially during the critical teenage years, may cost them (and you) more than they make.

You might want to communicate ownership of their rooms or of certain things under your roof (like their bikes or their toys). They need to have the option to use and even abuse these assets (short of blatant, willful sin). Such abuse should result in consequences, however. For example, leaving a bike out in the rain might result in not being able to ride it for a few days.

While we're on the subject of material assets, I need to mention an abuse parents often use. It's a subtle form of control, but it's control nonetheless. You may want to grab a roll of Tums before you read this.

Some children feel like their parents' personal slaves—especially older kids. Moms are notorious for turning their firstborn children into live-in nannies. In some cases, once a child is old enough to responsibly watch younger kids, moms hit the road and don't look back for the rest of their lives. It's typical for this kind of mom to simply announce her plans to the oldest child without giving him any notice or options.

"I'm going to the mall. Keep an eye on the kids."

If a friend came by your house, dropped off her children, and made the same announcement to you, how would you feel? Devalued? Used? Angry? That's what our children feel. Paul gave a strong admonition to fathers: *"Fathers, do not exasperate your children, that they may not lose heart"* (Colossians 3:21). That word *exasperate* literally means "to do something that causes them to resent you." It's great advice for both parents, and taking advantage of our children is just one way we can be guilty of violating it.

If we expect our older children to give us freedom to roam, we need to *pay* them. Obviously, however, there are exceptions to this rule. If Mom likes to go to the grocery story every Monday, for instance, she might set that afternoon aside for it. She could arrange with her oldest child to be available to watch the younger kids during that time. The baby-sitting responsibility would then fall under the category of "chores" and not require remuneration. After all, the oldest eats some of the food she's bringing home.

How do we know when to pay and when not to? Try asking yourself a few questions:

- If my oldest weren't here to watch the younger kids, would I normally pile the children into the car and go do this event (like grocery shopping)? If the answer is yes, that's an event you might want to put on the chore list. Abuse of this, however, will certainly build anger into your oldest.

- If my oldest weren't here to watch the younger kids, would I normally hire someone to watch the children or otherwise not go to this event (like a date with your spouse or an optional jaunt to the mall)? If the answer is yes in this case, fairness would dictate that it's your oldest's option, and that if he chooses to watch the kids, you should pay him. If you pay him less than you would your normal baby-sitter, he will assume you think he isn't as valuable, which is dishonoring to him. Also, if you pay him less, pretty soon he's going to be baby-sitting for your friends for more money, and you won't be able to hire him if you want to.

As I said before, however, we don't have to pay for everything. There's still plenty of room for chores to be done that are part of the privilege and responsibility of living within your family (cooking, cleaning, maintaining the yard, etc.). But we show grace when we remunerate our children for the genuine contributions they make that we consider above and beyond the call of duty.

- FUNCTIONAL ASSETS: Kids need help recognizing what their skills are, and then they need to be given outlets to develop those skills.

- INFORMATIONAL ASSETS: We need to give them liberal access to the things we know, as well as to create pipelines to the right sources for the things we don't know.

- SPIRITUAL ASSETS: Kids need to receive a depth of spiritual wisdom to turn to when needed. The best way to do this is by modeling our own spiritual growth and surrounding ourselves with mentors who can help us wisely lead our children. Kids need to be taught how to pray, how to find their way around the Bible, and how to get the most out of their church experience.

As painful as it may be, once they hit their teenage years, they should be given the option to choose their own church. The church *you* attend may not be meeting your children's needs. Forcing them to go to your church in that case, when there's a decent one down the street that would better suit them, is counterproductive. Logic says it doesn't make sense to compel teenagers to worship in one church when their hearts are in another. (I'm assuming that both churches teach Jesus and His Word.)

For the duration of their spiritual development under your roof, then, you may want to let your children go where God is leading them. And you may want occasionally to attend "their" church with them.

2. Build their expectations toward independence.

Let your children know you realize how much they want to call their own shots. Tell them you want to hand over that responsibility as quickly as possible. Since letting go is a gradual process, negotiate the areas of control that you can grant to them now. Let them know that the quicker they demonstrate responsibility in those areas, the quicker they will be given more control over other choices.

3. Give them an outlet to voice their frustration or disapproval of you.

Letting kids vent their feelings is not as threatening as it sounds. I was in McDonald's the other day and saw three different places where they had provided comment cards, something to write with, and a box in which to deposit your comments. The company was encouraging criticism. The reason is obvious: They want to be the best they can be, and they realize there is always room for improvement. Many of the upgrades to the services they render have come from this outlet for honesty.

We never seem to have any problem criticizing our children. If it doesn't go both ways, our criticism is undermined. But when they know they can vent their frustrations with us, they're more inclined to respond positively to our comments. They see them for what they are—information intended to make their lives more effective.

Every few months in the Kimmel home, we have "What's Your Beef Night." Each child gives Darcy his or her entrée order two days in advance, and we go to work preparing the menu. I might have a burger on the grill for Cody and a hotdog for Colt, while Darcy's cooking a pizza for Shiloh and paying for Chinese delivery at the front door for Karis. We sit down to dinner, and as the children enjoy their entrées, they get to "beef" about anything Darcy or I is doing that's bothering them.

Trust me, these have been some of the most exciting and eye-opening nights of our lives. Often we find out we've done things that we never knew had hurt them. The key to getting them to be honest is that we don't defend ourselves. They get a chance to ventilate without fear of reprisal.

A few days following "What's Your Beef Night," we have "What's Your Pleasure Night." That's where we all head to a restaurant known for having great desserts, and each kid gets to choose whatever dessert he or she wants. On this night, we go around the table and state the things we appreciate about each other. It's the icing on the cake!

Some children may have frustrations they don't feel comfortable stating in front of their siblings. We need to let them know they can come to us at any time about anything. After the first few times that they come to us and hear us assume responsibility *and apologize* for our actions against them, they'll know they can trust us with their emotions.

4. Prioritize what's important to them.

The things that are interesting to us may not be interesting to our children, but our kids are interesting and important to us. Therefore, we communicate grace when we appreciate what's interesting to them. We might have to do back flips over a piece of artwork we can't figure out or spend an hour listening to a CD we can't understand. But when they see that what interests them is important to us, they feel valued.

When the disciples returned to tell Jesus about the many things that happened when they were sent out two by two to proclaim His message, He already knew what they were going to say. Yet He hung on every word. He let them know how valuable they were to Him by His interest in the fine points of their lives.[3]

5. Build them up to others.

Soft soap is about 80 percent lye, but genuine praise is solid gold. Paul commended Timothy to the Philippians. He sang his praises and prepared the Philippians for Timothy's ministry. His kind words did more for Timothy than anything else could have.

6. Pray for them daily, and communicate to them that you're doing it.

When kids know their moms and dads are faithfully upholding them in prayer, it gives them a great deal of assurance. They grow to count on it.

They can also get some confidence that if you're talking to God about them every day, He might be talking to you about how you're dealing with them.

7. Give them the freedom to be unique.

One of the best ways to keep our controlling tendencies in check is by granting our children the freedom to be different—to make room for their quirks. This is one of the most freeing actions a loving parent can take. And children loved for their uniqueness just might surprise you. If I've enjoyed any success as an adult, I attribute it primarily to parents who accepted me as I was and encouraged me to develop my quirks!

I close this discussion with one of my favorite poems about children. For the mom and dad who want to empower their children, these words by poet Digby Wolfe say it all . . .

Here's to the Kids Who Are Different

Here's to the kids who are different,
The kids who don't always make A's.
The kids who have ears twice the size of their peers,
And noses that go on for days.

Here's to the kids who are different,
The kids they call "stupid" and "dumb."
The kids who aren't cute and don't give a hoot,
Who march to a different drum.

Here's to the kids who are different,
The kids with a mischievous streak.
For when they have grown, as history has shown,
It's their difference that makes them unique.[4]

To your kids and mine, salute.

CHAPTER 15

Overcontrolling In-Laws

Some parents wrap a noose around their children's potential when they're little and never take it off. Some parents not only maintain control over their children after the kids have left home, but they continue it long after they're in their graves.

A woman came home from the funeral of her high-control mother, took dishes down from the cupboards, and set them all over the counter. She got butter and jelly out of the refrigerator and smeared it all over them. Then she proceeded to stack them in the sink. Next she went into the living room and shifted the cushions on the sofa to make them crooked. She tilted paintings and lamp shades, broke a candle into little pieces, and threw its wax all over the carpet. She went into the children's rooms, pulled down the covers on their beds, and threw clothing from their closets throughout the room. When her son walked in to see what was going on, she put her fingers in his hair and mussed it until clumps stood up straight.

"There, I've shown her," she said. "She can't run my life anymore."

But the facts say differently. In reality, her mother was doing an excellent job of pulling her daughter's strings from six feet under. This lady's behavior was bizarre and inappropriate. And it was a direct way of trying to prove something that wasn't and probably never would be true for a long

175

time. She didn't have control over her own life.

Running our kids' lives can do a lot of damage when they're little, but it can destroy them when they're older. It puts them in a position where they find it difficult to grow up. Some never do. It can also destroy the key relationships in their lives. We can all tell stories of marriages that came apart at the seams primarily because of overcontrolling in-laws and parents.

When In-laws Become Outlaws

Being an in-law, like parenting, is a sacred trust. It's an opportunity to stand aside and let our children take over the reins of their lives. It's a chance to move into a position of adviser, mentor, and sounding board. But it's imperative that we don't step over that line.

When I went away to college, a man selling life insurance set up shop in the lounge of our dormitory and pitched his product to us guys. When I'd heard his presentation, I had more questions than answers. When he tried to clarify some of his terminology, he confused me even more. But there was no doubt what he wanted when he turned the application around and held the pen out to me. It was time for me to make my first "adult" purchase. I balked.

I needed more information, and I knew where to get it. That night, I called my father and tried my best to explain the options that had been thrown my way.

In a few minutes, he gave me a short course on life insurance as well as on life. He provided enough information that I could make an intelligent decision. Then he made his final point. "Tim, you make the call. You're the one who has to make the premium payments, so take this information and do what you think is best."

My father didn't tell me how to run my finances. He simply helped me understand the options and left the decision with me. Too often, parents continue to bankroll their children for years after they're married, and in the process they maintain a say in how the kids' money is spent. They keep their children both dependent and lame. When this happens, one or both parties develop resentment toward the other.

Let's grab our Bibles and wander around in a familiar text. It's the one we hear a lot at weddings, as well we should. It not only serves as a superb checklist for successful marriages, but it also outlines the parameters that can protect the relationship between the new couple and their parents.

For this cause a man shall leave his father and his mother, and shall cleave to his wife; and they shall become one flesh. And the man and his wife were both naked and were not ashamed.
Genesis 2:24-25

First things first: We need to keep in mind whom God was saying this to when He said it the first time. It was spoken to Adam and Eve who had no physical parents, but became the first parents on earth.

In other words, before they knew what a mother and father was, God taught them what a mother and father's biggest job would be. In a nutshell, they are supposed to *let their children go.* It's great if, when that time comes, we have groomed them for independence. Regardless of their maturity or ability, we're to let the two people become one entity—a new limb on the family tree with the freedom to grow whichever way they want.

As a father, I can't think of anything that could be more frightening—except the alternative. What happens too often is that parents maintain some tie to their children that enables them to exercise undue influence. It may be financial, social, spiritual, or emotional. What they create in the process, more often than not, is a marital monster.

Colonel Mom and Major Dad

One woman told me that when she made love to her husband, she felt his mother's presence in the bed with them. His mother maintained such an intense hold on his heartstrings that there was hardly a thing happening between them that she didn't both know about and have an opinion on. That included their sexual relationship. As a result, the wife was finding it difficult to respond intimately to her husband.

Once at a wedding rehearsal dinner, a father got up to toast his daughter and future son-in-law. He informed all of us that as far as he was concerned, nothing was going to change in his relationship with his daughter. She was simply getting a partner, not leaving home.

I knew this man and his reputation well. The hard-nosed, spit-in-your-eye control he exercised in the business community had lifted him to the position of chief executive officer in a substantial company. Unfortunately, he used the same methods of control on his children. The debris from his other kids' wrecked marriages was all around me at the table. I was sitting across from one of his divorced daughters when he made his "Me Tarzan, you Cheetah" speech to his son-in-law. She whispered loudly enough to be heard, "That #!*. He'd better not destroy *this* marriage."

God told Adam and Eve that when a couple marries, they are to discontinue their dependency on their parents and bond with each other instead. They are to turn to each other for the emotional, social, moral, physical, and financial support their relationship requires. It's been written in a million books, but it can't be written enough: God expects a couple to gain from each other what they formerly gained from their parents. This assumes two strategic points:

1. that they are willing to leave their parents.
2. that their parents are willing to let them go.

I often see couples who desire to honor their parents and each other by developing their own life together, but the parents won't ease up on their influence. Sometimes Mom and Dad even quote Scripture to remind them how they are to "honor and obey" their parents. The biblical way to honor parents when we become adults, however, is by relinquishing them from any financial and emotional responsibilities on the day we are married, and by being committed to provide for their financial needs should they require help in their old age. The obligation to obey our parents ceases the day we get married. From that day forward, we are to develop a richer and deeper relationship with them as an adult married couple.

This is next to impossible if parents won't cooperate. I've watched parents intimidate their married children into continuing their attendance at the church where they grew up, even though the couple didn't feel that church now met their needs. Hiding behind the Bible, the parents exercised undue pressure in order to keep their children close. Maybe the parents' reason for coercing the newly married couple was that they loved to see them on Sunday. That's fine, but it's not the parents' call.

Purse Strings

Without doubt, the most effective way parents continue to control their children after they leave home is with money. Today's economy is unmerciful to young couples. Few come to matrimony with large sums of money, and because of their limited credit history, they find it difficult to borrow from the bank. Parents are often the natural—and sometimes only—resource for seed money. Some parents are able to loan money, but few can either loan it or give it without tying a network of strings around it. They've bought into the idea that he who provides the gold gets to make the rules.

God isn't against parents' helping their children make a down payment on a house or get a business started, but He is against those parents' using their money to manipulate their children. Loaning our children money for a house doesn't entitle us to dictate how they wallpaper it. All of this type of coercion brings strife where there's supposed to be love and harmony.

Grace-Based In-laws

God blesses parents who let their children grow up to be independent. He increases their standing in their children's eyes and gives them joy in their old age. But if we disobey Him regarding our grown children, He allows the consequences of our meddling and control to haunt us throughout the rest of our lives—even to our last days. Too many funerals have been a climax of regret. Families where parents have refused to let their children develop independence have seen brother turn against brother and sisters refuse to speak to each other for years. *What a shame! And what a waste of love!*

We can be revered patriarchs and matriarchs if we bring our children to the threshold of independence and then let them pass over without us to the challenges awaiting them on the other side. They still remain our children. We are still loved as their parents. We're simply letting them sprout wings and fly.

Mothers and fathers who have already harmed their kids through overcontrol can still play a big role in rectifying the pain. If this is true of your parenting, three steps can make all the difference in the world. Those steps are:

Admit wrong: Acknowledge to them that you realize you've been exercising harmful influence in their lives. Be specific about how you've been doing it. Don't be surprised if they add to your list.

Repent your wrong: Ask them to forgive you. Take full responsibility for the damage your control may have done to their marriage or children. Seek forgiveness from the Lord, too. Identify your sinful control to Him, and ask for His mercy and help in repairing the damage.

Stop doing it: The only way to demonstrate your sincerity is by getting out of their emotional, spiritual, or financial way and letting God build them as they put their trust in Him.

For Those in Bondage to Their Parents or In-laws

We all know that it's easier to talk about breaking away from the high-control ties of our parents-in-law than it is to actually do it. But couples who are struggling from the oppression of overbearing parents and in-laws may have to take some frightening but essential steps.

1. *Acknowledge what your parents or in-laws are doing.* Rather than maintaining partisan lines, honestly assess the way your parents' or in-laws' interference in the life of your family is harming everyone involved. This may require a husband's admitting that his mother is hurting his wife.

2. *Confront them.* Lovingly but honestly, tell them you understand what they're doing, that you don't like it, and that you want to figure out a peaceful solution.

3. *Ask them for the blessing of independence.* Honor them by giving them the opportunity to back out of their controlling posture, keeping their dignity intact. Let them know how much you love them and need their gift of freedom. Tell them how much you want to respond to them

as patriarch and matriarch of the family, and how much easier that will be once they have allowed you to live as an independent person. Acknowledge that you will make mistakes but that their grace-based gift of independence will be the best way to help you learn from them.

4. *If they won't discontinue their controlling tendencies, take drastic measures.*

A family in the East learned how painful but essential this step was. Four siblings grew up, married, and had children. They remained in the same area as their parents and enjoyed a healthy and encouraging relationship with them—that is, until Thanksgiving came. Then the control would begin. Multiple sets of in-laws used guilt and shame to coerce the children into eating Thanksgiving dinner at the "old homestead." That served as a warm-up for the war that would rage for the next month. Each set of in-laws felt their children should celebrate Christmas "where you've opened your presents every Christmas since your childhood."

The problem was obvious: Four siblings, four couples, five sets of in-laws, two holidays. You can't be everyplace at once. Packing the kids and all the stuff they require was turning the holidays into a nightmare. After a half-dozen years of this, the couples began to see that all of this was driving a wedge between spouses, children, and in-laws. It had long ago thrown a damper over the holidays for them.

Most families don't allow this kind of nightmare to happen. But these families had parents who weren't willing to let go of the past. Ultimately, the four couples had a meeting. All shared their frustrations and found their feelings were almost identical. The holidays had become something they dreaded. That's when they decided to confront their parents. They were going to start celebrating the holidays in whatever way they felt best for their children. They welcomed the grandparents to join in whichever way they wanted. But one thing was left clear: They were going to start developing their own individual family traditions. Their marriages and children needed it.

Three years later, one set of parents finally came around. Meanwhile, each couple had developed some wonderful traditions for their own children—and stopped a lot of pain between themselves. In the years that followed, they occasionally celebrated the holidays at "the homestead." The parents ultimately recognized their children had been right. It all pivoted on some courage.

Solving a problem like where you eat Christmas dinner may seem minor compared to some of the painful conflicts with which you have to deal. Your parents may be foisting controls on you that cannot be settled without fierce emotional pain on both sides. You may have to face angry or bitter words, accusations, silence, or punishment. You may have turn your back on certain emotional or financial benefits. You may have to move away.

It's unfortunate that so much pain has to accompany a relationship that God expected to be a haven of a loving support. But sometimes people refuse to obey God. And sometimes those close to them have to pay a big price for it. But God honors those who lovingly do what's right. Removing yourself from the proximity of high-control in-laws doesn't mean you don't love or respect them. It does mean, however, that you are willing to carry out your stewardship before God and not allow their high control to infect your marriage.

For those who trust God on this matter, He promises much gain.

You will seek Me and find Me, when you search for Me with all your heart.

Jeremiah 29:13

CHAPTER 16

Evangelical Power Brokers

"Y ou can't put those out."

"What?"

"That brochure there—you can't set that out on the table." The gentleman talking to me was pastor of a church that had brought me in to speak to its parents. The brochure he was talking about was for a weekend marriage conference that would soon be coming to their town. It was sponsored by a national Christian organization. I appreciate this marriage ministry's work. Their material is rock solid, practical, and biblically sound. I figured some of the people at my parenting workshop would benefit greatly from this conference. So during a break in one of my sessions, I was stacking a couple dozen brochures on a resource table at the back of the room. When the pastor saw what I was doing, he came over to make his statement.

"Do you mean you don't want me to put them here, or you don't want me to put them anywhere?" I asked.

He had caught me so off guard with his statement that I initially thought he was intending a better location for them.

"You can't put them anywhere, Tim," he answered. "I don't *allow* my people to go to that conference."

Some words bring out the worst in people. Like someone sliding his fingernails down a chalkboard, those words seem to grab your focus and raise the hair on the back of your neck. This pastor had put the right words together to make me react.

"I'm not sure I'm following you," I said. "Did you say you don't *allow* your people to attend this marriage conference?"

"That's right. It goes through Sunday, and on Sunday my people belong in the worship service here. This church is to be the source of their teaching. I just don't allow them to go to that kind of 'outsider' gathering. Plus, they might use their tithe to pay for it. They should be giving their tithe to this church—not some parachurch organization."

"Pastor, are you familiar with the content of this conference?"

"No, but it doesn't matter."

"Well, I'm very familiar with it, and I can testify that it's as solid biblically as you could want. It's like a couple getting to take 'Successful Marriage 101.' The mileage the people of this church would gain is beyond calculation. Marriages would be strengthened, and struggling marriages would be healed. Families would be stronger. Plus, it would save you a lot of time by lightening your marriage counseling load. I've heard the testimonies from lots of the couples who have attended it. God has really used this conference to give hope to homes all across America. And as far as the tithe issue goes, I know for a fact that the speakers at this conference consistently remind the couples not to forget to give their offerings back at their home church."

"I'm sorry, Tim, but I don't permit my people to attend. You can't make the brochures available."

I complied. I was his guest; he was the pastor. But I was still bristling from those inflammatory words: "I don't *allow my people.*"

Sinners in the Hands of an Angry Preacher

That pastor was what I call an evangelical power broker. Cloaked in the mantle of the prophet, with an ordination certificate on the wall and a Bible under his arm, he was holding a congregation under siege through some misguided understanding of his authority. Fortunately, he doesn't represent the majority of pastors. But he does represent a destructive minority. He stood with too many other men who think their call to ministry gives them title to make decisions for their people.

Since our churches are mere extensions of our homes, and our homes are mere extensions of our churches, it's necessary that I address a chapter to the leaders of our churches. The churches we attend should be bolstering the spiritual life of our homes. And because we are there, our grace-based families should be bringing a rich heritage to our fellow believers. But our best intentions can run amuck if we attend churches with pastors, elders, deacons, or teachers who wield undue authority in our families' lives.

Sermonator or Terminator

It's nothing short of amazing what some Christian leaders feel is their prerogative when it comes to the people who sit under their teaching. Some pastors feel they can tell their people which way to vote, whom they can marry, how many children they can have, where they should work, how they are to educate their children, how much money they have to give to the church, where they must serve, and how often they must be in church. But there's something that we who have ordination certificates need to make sure we understand about the stewardship we've been given:

> **God left us in charge of His message...**
> **but He did not leave us in charge of His people.**

God alone is in charge of His people. His way of dealing with His children is through grace. He makes it clear where the boundaries are; He gives lots of room for each person's individuality, and then He gives them all the freedom to decide what they're going to do. Truth plays a big part in all this. As Jesus taught us, by knowing the truth, we will be set free.[1] God loves His children enough to let them live by faith.

Leaders who assume responsibility for their people's individual choices bring sickness to the flock. Rather than preaching and teaching

God's truth and letting the Holy Spirit convict them, they feel they have the authority to serve as the Holy Spirit on the people's behalf. Such action is spiritual tyranny. Christian leaders who carry on this way place their churches in an extremely vulnerable position with the forces of darkness. Satan has gained a beachhead in many churches through the abuse of power by God's leadership and the broken hearts they've left in their wake.

Pastors and teachers have an awesome list of responsibilities to God and His flock. But those leaders need to remember they are stewards, not owners; shepherds, not warlords. One of their responsibilities is to teach God's truth. They are also to minister to the physical, emotional, and spiritual needs of the congregation. They have been mandated to set standards and boundaries, as well as to administer consequences if certain boundaries are crossed.

A pastor may refuse to marry a couple, for example, because he can show them how their union would be in direct violation of God's teaching. But he can't forbid them to get married. He is to bring God's Word to bear upon their hearts, but it's up to them to either honor or reject the message.

Pastors are to plead God's cause, show people the way to heaven, and search for them when they wander off. They, along with the leaders of the church, might even have to administer church discipline to a parishioner who is involved in odious sin.

Pastors can also apply God's truth to various issues that cross spiritual and political lines. They can do their best to inform the congregation of the moral consequences that might accompany certain political issues. But the Bible is not a "politically correct" piece of literature, and Christianity must not bow to political elitists who try to redefine the gospel. So pastors must be bold to state the truth, in love, regardless of whether it's popular. But how people vote is up to them.

When a pastor forbids people to get married, make an investment, have a television set, go to a particular college, or have only so many children, he's doing far more than playing God—he's playing *against* God. There is no way he or the work to which he's attached can count on receiving God's blessing.

Strident, legalistic teaching is a popular form of control. Churches where pastors have been abusive in this way are filled with brokenhearted worshipers. There's nothing wrong with teaching biblical absolutes. Pastors are expected to serve as a conscience to the people. They are to apply God's Word with a conviction that pricks the hearts of people who are living disobediently. But legalism is different. It becomes a substitute for the Holy Spirit, a vehicle that enables spiritually proud coercion to propagate itself.

An honest appraisal of high-control pastors and Christian workers shows they are typically motivated by the same things outlined earlier: fear, anger, shame, and bondage.

Fear: Scripture teaches that God has not given us a spirit of fear but of power, love, and discipline. Yet some Christian leaders are seized with fear. It fuels the flames of distrust. It clouds their reasoning. It leads them to professional paranoia. The power plays that go on among pastors within the same church often have their roots in this unfortunate and discouraging emotion.

I need to acknowledge at this point that a certain amount of fear could grip even the most righteous servant. When you gain your living from service to God's cause, you have one of the most secure careers you can find. Your future is guaranteed by none other than the Creator of the universe. However, you have one of the most *insecure* job situations on this planet. Flocks are fickle. Our churches are filled with consumer-oriented Christians. They approach Sunday like a trip to the mall. If they don't like what they see, they'll go down the street to the church with the living Christmas tree and brass section. Yuppie Christians like to be impressed. Their unrealistic expectations cause them to get extremely upset when their pastors—preaching God's Word diligently—happen to hammer on their particular brand of disobedience.

In addition, deacons and elders have a bad habit of waving a paycheck under the pastor's nose and telling him to jump through hoops that compromise his calling from God or the best interests of the congregation. When you also consider that Christian workers are notoriously shortchanged on payday, you can understand how, if you were wearing the clerical collar, you'd struggle with fear, too.

But the fact remains that no fear justifies our assuming control in other Christians' lives.

Anger: The pulpit is an excellent platform for ventilating hostility. But there is righteous anger and unrighteous anger. Humble servanthood demands that we never allow unrighteous anger to turn our platforms into bully pulpits. Sometimes the pastor is angry at God. Because he's either unable to see it or unwilling to admit it, he can find himself stepping over that thin line and seizing responsibility for his congregation's choices.

Shame: In the past few years, we've seen several high-visibility preachers who were known for their throat-hold style of leadership brought down by shameful sin. When I'm allowed close to the hearts of Christian workers who wield overbearing control on the people around them, too often I find some painful past that haunts them.

As a seminary student, I came to realize that too many of my fellow students were preparing for the ministry for cathartic reasons. They'd fallen short in some area of their lives and sinned. Their training for ministry was their way of salving the wounds caused by their guilt and shame. That approach doesn't work. Christ's shed blood on the cross is the answer to guilt and shame. A couple of those classmates come to my mind even as I write this. Those sad men didn't last long in the ministry. And their demise was all the more unfortunate because of the innocent people who went down with them.

Bondage: A series of wrong choices, made over a long enough period, can cauterize our wills and consciences. When that happens, we find ourselves in bondage to our urges, lusts, and greed. Control is a standard way this plays itself out. I've worked side by side in ministry with men addicted to control. They couldn't function without dominating the personal choices of those in the foxhole with them. Those times when I've had to work so closely with such power brokers were true dark days in my professional life.

Holding Everything You Have in an Open Palm

Darcy and I consider ourselves extremely blessed. If we were to list the things we consider our greatest treasures, our local church would be near the top of the list. There are several reasons God is blessing our church, but I think the primary one is our pastor. Darryl loves God, God's people, and God's Word. Like so many men and women who serve God vocationally, Darryl brings humility and grace to his role. But he brings something else as well. Let me give you two examples.

Darcy signed up to work in the nursery. A few weeks later, she got a letter from Pastor Darryl. Paraphrasing it, he said, "Darcy, I'm so glad to see that you'll be working in the nursery over the next six months. You're the type of woman we love to have working with our children. As you know, we have two services on Sunday morning. You'll be in the nursery for one of them. For the other one, you have a choice between attending your Sunday school class or coming to the worship service. I want to encourage you to go to your Sunday school class. As much as I'd enjoy having you in the preaching service, the fact remains that your Sunday school class is better equipped to meet your needs."

The second example comes from something Darryl does frequently. He'll approach the pulpit bubbling with excitement, like a kid with a secret he can't wait to tell. "I've got somebody I want you to meet," he'll say when he reaches the microphone. At that point, a couple will walk up on the platform to join him.

These couples are pastors and their wives from churches, either newly planted or established, located in the communities surrounding our church. In other words, these pastors minister to the exact same group of believers from which our church draws. Darryl usually has the wife tell about their family. Then he has the pastor describe his vision for the community or his church. Darryl has even been known to step aside and let the visiting pastor give the message for that service.

Next, Darryl puts his arms around the couple and leads us all in prayer for their marriage, their children, and their work. But how he concludes really shows you where his security lies. Here's what he says to his congregation: "These servants need help, and some of you need to team up with them. Look deeply into your heart. Is God tugging? If so, I want to encourage you to head on over to their church next Sunday, roll up your sleeves, and get involved helping them reach our community."

You know what? People take him up on it. They walk out the door of our church and transfer their spiritual gifts, financial resources, and devotion to those other churches. But for every family that walks out the door, God brings five others to take its place.

Darryl holds his gifts in an open palm. He also holds his pulpit, his calling, and the people who worship with him the same way. Maybe that explains the phenomenal growth of our church. Thousands of people crowd our campus to bask under his grace-driven ministry. Often they're shocked to hear Darryl praying for his colleagues ministering in churches just down the street. They aren't used to a pastor who is that secure. But Darryl understands what I wish all of us in the ministry understood:

> **We own nothing; it's all God's. We're called to be faithful stewards of what He's entrusted to us, and we're to let God Almighty have the glory.**

Few passages of Scripture sum up this principle as well as 1 Peter 5:1-7. Listen to how God's Spirit so poetically preaches to the heart of the pastor:

> *Therefore, I exhort the elders among you, as your fellow elder and witness of the sufferings of Christ, and a partaker of the glory that is to be revealed, shepherd the flock of God among you, exercising oversight not under compulsion, but voluntarily, according to the will of God; and not for sordid gain, but with eagerness; nor yet as lording it over those allotted to your charge, but proving to be examples to the flock. And when the Chief Shepherd appears, you will receive the unfading crown of glory. You younger men, likewise, be subject to your elders; and all of you, clothe yourselves with humility toward one another, for God is opposed to the proud, but gives grace to the humble.*

We've been called to manage, not muscle; to constrain, not coerce. The people in the church are His, not ours. And when we hold all He has given us in an open palm, He is not only free to use us, but also to empower the precious people He allows us to serve.

When the Sheep Grow Teeth

I would be remiss if I left this discussion of evangelical power brokers without also looking at the issues from the other side of the communion table. The man behind the pulpit makes a big target, and some people have no shame in the way they take shots at him and his family. Some pastors walk into crossfire and crawl away so wounded that they never recover the joy they need to meet God's call. As I speak in churches across the country, I'm amazed at how many pastors, pastors' wives, and pastors' children nurse broken hearts.

I hear the complaints from the saints. I hear them desperately trying to justify the severe attacks they make on the servants God has brought to their church. Sometimes genuine problems exist that need to be addressed. But the treatment I've seen some pastors take at the hands of high-control elders, deacons, or other leaders makes me sick to my stomach. I look past the pastor to his sons and daughters and see children beaten down because they love their parents but are helpless to protect them. I look at the self-righteous leaders using the Bible and the sentiments of like-minded people to justify their disgraceful treatment of God's servants.

When I see these things, I think of the scriptural passage that talks about what happens to people who selfishly attack God's anointed servants. I also think of the coming day when those unreasonable accusers must stand before God and give an account for their actions. Their only hope will be that they'll stand before a God of grace. Abusive control of God's workers is blatant disrespect of the Lord Himself.

Some churches have languished for decades without God's blessing because of the way they've treated their pastors without realizing the harm they were doing. Often it's only a few individuals in the congregation who are at fault, and the rest of the people in the pews have been victimized by the few.

We know from Scripture that this happens. The entire Israelite army suffered because one man had allowed sin into the camp.[2] If the Israelites had failed to rectify his sin, they would have continued to suffer corporately. The failure to correct the sin of the few against a pastor or fellow parishioner may cause the entire flock to be held responsible.

But there's hope. Many churches have learned the hard way about the abuse of control. We can benefit from their mistakes. I want to close this chapter with two letters I recently received. They're letters that were exchanged between a brokenhearted pastor and his former church. I've changed the names and locations to protect the innocent and the guilty. But these letters demonstrate how painful overcontrol can be, as well as how God longs to have His children apply His grace to rectify the wrong.

The first letter is to the Reverend Brown (the heartbroken pastor) from the church he used to serve. The follow-up letter is his response to the congregation's grace.

Grab a box of Kleenex, and read how a congregation brought life back to the family of a beaten-down servant.

Dear Pastor Brown:

The purpose of this letter is to seek your forgiveness, and to reconcile and restore the relationship between you and your wife and the members of our church body here at First Church.

During the past months, the elder board of First Church has discussed and prayed about the circumstances that led to your resignation. Pastor Jones, in his June 30 message, explained that sins committed by a small group of people in positions of authority within a church can become "corporate" sins that negatively affect the entire church. One thing became apparent from his message: When these types of corporate sins are committed, they need to be confessed. We, as a congregation, sense a need to seek your forgiveness.

Our understanding of events in 1986 is incomplete; those who were in elder positions in 1986 are no longer with us at First Church. With the exception of three families, no one within our body has any firsthand knowledge of the situation. Review of the official record has provided little insight. Your letter of resignation is the most extensive document from that time.

However, based upon the information available to us, we acknowledge the following:

The complaints against you were largely unspecified and unfocused. Immorality or doctrinal error was never at issue.

In your letter of resignation, your desire for reconciliation is clearly stated. Issues that you felt were offenses against the body were confessed, and a request for forgiveness from the body was made. Further, based upon this and other information, we are convinced that every attempt to love and support you as our pastor and to resolve whatever difficulties were occurring was not made in full. Please forgive us for failing you.

The proper treatment of church leaders and pastors is outlined in 1 Thessalonians 5:12-13:

But we request of you, brethren, that you appreciate those who diligently labor among you, and have charge over you in the Lord and give you instruction, and that you esteem them very highly in love because of their work. Live in peace with one another.

Currently we love, honor, and appreciate Pastor John Jones and his wife, Pamela. We assume the best of them and strive within our leadership team, and the body as a whole, for a trusting and united spirit in working with one another. Our sense is that the appreciation, esteem, and honor you deserved as our pastor, and the desire to establish a unified ministry team that included you, was at some point allowed to slip away. As a result, the desire for reconciliation, mutual encouragement, and mutual trust was also in part absent. In this failing, we have sinned against you and ask you to forgive us.

Further, even if the difficulties were indeed irreconcilable, we as a church did not handle the situation with the love and sensitivity that should have occurred. Our failure in this area included events prior to and after your resignation. As an example, our understanding is that only a very few individuals from our body assisted you in packing for your move. In spite of the awkwardness that may have resulted from the situation, our obligation to you and your family to provide love and

193

encouragement remained. Instead, our relationship was cut off abruptly, perhaps because of hard feelings or because the situation made things "uncomfortable." Please forgive us for our callousness to you and your family.

At the conclusion of Pastor Jones's message on Sunday, June 30, we prayed as a congregation, including a time of confession. The quarterly business meeting followed. At the close of that meeting, a motion was made and seconded to write you this letter to confess the sin of our church family against you as our first pastor and to seek your forgiveness. The motion passed unanimously.

We very much would like to have you visit us the next time you are out here, and invite you to minister to us from the pulpit, to preach a sermon of healing and forgiveness. (Please let us know when you will be out this way so proper preparations can be made.)

We look forward to hearing from you. May the Lord continue to bless you and your family!

Sincerely in Christ,

The First Church Family

(Signed by all church members and regular attendees present the Sunday before being mailed.)

Now here is Pastor Brown's reply:

Dear Pastor Jones, Leadership, and Body,

Betty and I received your letter of July 21. We must tell you that at first there was a foreboding sense of fear as to why you would contact us, especially with a certified letter. As we read the letter, we were astonished at what we were reading. Deep within our hearts, a clutching grip of pain began to release its hold on our spirits. The first few days were spent reading and rereading your letter and looking at each other in wonder, joy, and disbelief, thinking anything so good couldn't be real. For you to understand how we felt when we received your letter, you must understand some of the things we experienced during our time at First Church and our subsequent leaving.

We had no idea that the pain, so old, still exercised such a viselike hold on our memories and our daily lives. We decided that we would not share our hurt with our new church as we did not want to bring the events of the past with us. Perhaps this was unwise; I do not know. The depressions and grief lasted three years, as well as the lack of self-confidence, self-esteem, and the fear of failure that I developed as a pastor and as a person. For several of those years, we wrote letters to people at First Church pouring out our pain and grief, and then we destroyed them. We never mailed those letters for fear of how they might be received and not wanting to chance any more hurt. Thus, the pain remained sealed in our spirits.

The main reason stated for requesting my resignation was the lack of joy in my preaching. The elders informed me that I did not make people feel good in my sermons, and thus the church was cold and unfriendly. I was informed that joy was a fruit of the Holy Spirit and cannot be lacking from the pastor's life. After several years of nonstop effort, I grew discouraged by the expectations, exhaustion of planting a church, conflict between several elders, lack of cooperation between elders, infighting, blame shifting, arguing, and lack of pastor support amongst the leadership team. This was the source of the lack of joy that I was experiencing.

I had a trusted mentor listen to several of my tapes to help me evaluate them and grow. He did not find this lack of joy but praised my preaching and encouraged me to continue. However, the elders expressed concern that I had stayed too long and that it was time for me to leave. I told them that I stayed so long because faithfulness is a fruit of the Holy Spirit.

When they asked me to resign, I was informed that this was the general consensus of the church. I found out later this was not true, but I felt, at the time, that if the body did not want me, obviously I could not continue my ministry. When the elders came to my home and demanded my resignation, they told me I would not appear before the body again. With that, my heart as a shepherd was broken. I had many deep love relationships in the flock. Some asked us why we did not fight. Betty and I made a decision that, like Christ, we would not respond to our detractors. I do not mean to sound super-spiritual by that, as I knew in my heart that I was anything but super-spiritual. At that point I was just a very confused and hurting person.

I informed the elders that the previous weekend I had candidated at another church. I told them that the candidate weekend went exceptionally well, and I felt they would call me as pastor. I asked them if rather than resigning we could have a very gentle transition by my accepting this call, gentle for the body and gentle for me as a pastor. I assured them I would be very circumspect in anything I said to the congregation. They informed me that this was not possible. To maintain integrity with the other church, I called them that evening and informed them of what had just occurred. Their conclusion was to discontinue my candidacy.

As you know from my letter of resignation, our son came under a tremendous amount of criticism for his behavior. The leadership of that time criticized our parenting of him. The church chairman instructed us that we needed to "smack him more." We were also told that, according to the teaching of a national seminar speaker on relationships within the family, when parents discipline a child and he does not obey, it is because of unconfessed sin in the parents' lives. During an annual perform-ance evaluation, two elders decided to include my son in the review. I informed them that my son was not an employee of the church and should not be included in a performance review. They insisted and instructed me that his behavior was not acceptable and that in accordance to the qualifications of an elder, I did not have my family under control. This is the response of hurt and anger you find in my letter of resignation. I informed them that if I did not meet the qualifications of an elder, I did not qualify to be their pastor.

Upon moving here, we met a very godly neurologist who was the former head of the pediatric behavioral medicine program at the medical center. After evaluating our son, he determined that he suffered severely with a recently discovered neurological disability called Brain Stem Dyacontrol Syndrome. The brain stem controls all of a person's emotional actions, hyperactivity, the mental ability to determine such things as right from wrong, and anger. He reassured us our son was a very good and wonderful boy and that we were not bad parents. We were informed that his disability was the result of a missing neuro-hormone that was replaceable. Our son began taking the medicine and within six months was a completely transformed child. The doctor asked if we wanted him to write a letter to the First Church explaining these things, but we declined, not wanting to stir up the anguish but to put it behind us.

Prior to the beginning of my ministry at First Church, I was extensively criticized by one elder for purchasing a home computer with my own funds on which I did all the work of the church. During the ninety days following my resignation, the elders stopped my severance pay and demanded that I remove the church database from my home computer and allow them to search the files within my computer in order to remove anything that they deemed the property of the church. I, of course, refused them access.

These events and our subsequent move were followed by several years of emotional darkness, great self-doubt, deep anguish, tears, and many nights just holding Betty and wiping away her tears. She, through her pain, went on a crusade to relentlessly encourage me, over and over again building me up as a pastor and man of God.

I cannot begin to express to you the unbelievable blessings and release your letter bring to us. I think the greatest feeling we experienced was a wonderful, deep sense of freedom. The grip of self-doubt, guilt, and failure began to loosen its hold. We had no idea it would affect us so much. My parents were also deeply moved by your letter. We have shared it with many others. We will keep it and reread it for many years to come. Because of your sensitivity to the Holy Spirit, the Scriptures, and the teaching of Pastor Jones, you have ministered to us in an unbelievable manner.

It is with great joy that Betty and I express to you our complete forgiveness. To lay down this burden lightens our hearts immeasurably. Your graciousness in writing to us demonstrates your desire for godliness and the godliness of your leadership. Pastor Jones and Pamela must be extraordinary people. You are blessed to have them. Stand firmly behind them. Pastors and their wives are nothing but ordinary people trying to do an extraordinary job. I greatly appreciated your statement in your letter that you "...always assume the best of him." This is so important. I cannot help but think that Christ must be exceedingly pleased with First Church. I know we are.

I loved you when I was your pastor. I have continued to love you all throughout the years, and I still love you now. Many were the times I wished I could return to First Church and preach. I have much I want to share with you to help you grow. And now to actually receive an invitation is a dream come true. I graciously accept. Until the time when I can fulfill your gracious invitation, please know that before the witness of our eternal Father and the Lord Jesus Christ, you are completely forgiven! Go in peace, win the lost, and disciple the saved.

Your letter to me was dated July 21. You might be interested to know that July 21 happens to be my birthday. God gave me a very generous birthday gift in the form of your letter. He is gracious. Thank you, First Church, for the wonderful present.

Under His mercy,

Pastor Brown

Closing the Book on the Past

Maybe God is speaking to you right now. Maybe you participated—or sat by watching helplessly—while one of God's servants became a sacrificial lamb. It's never too late to give grace. For many of you reading this, God can't wait to restore His blessing to you and your church. I've been praying for you while writing. I've whispered it for all of you who need to make things right with the people who have been abused. I've prayed that God will empower you to do what's right. Be strong and courageous.

CHAPTER 17

Coping with a High Controller

Tony adjusted the cylinder so that the bullet would turn to the firing chamber as the hammer came down. Sitting in his closet, surrounded by his wife's clothing, he couldn't understand how, after all these years, it could evaporate so quickly. One day he was married, enjoying his relationship with the woman he had awakened next to for more than 20 years. The next day, he found himself staring at divorce papers.

No explanation. She refused to talk about it. Just, "I've had it. I can't take it anymore. If I don't get out of this relationship, I'm going to go crazy—if I'm not there already."

She told him she'd give him three days to find another place to stay, and then she wanted him to move out. Other than that, she refused to communicate. She said that all his control tactics would come out in court. For now, she just wanted him out of her sight.

I'll make it permanent, he said to himself. Sitting Indian style on the floor of their walk-in closet seemed to him an inappropriate posture for his last moment on earth. There was no muck and mire handy, so this would have to do. His hand lifted the revolver to the side of his temple, and his eyes automatically squeezed tightly shut.

"Tony? Tony! Are you in there? Tony, open up. I know you're in there. What are you doing?"

Waiting Too Long

As Tony recounted this story to me in a hotel coffee shop, he kept stroking his wife's hand. She sat next to him, listening as he outlined how their relationship had deteriorated to such a hopeless level. Sherry was a quiet person who had become a defiant woman through years of painful control tactics by her husband. When her emotions finally hit their kindling point, she felt the only solution was to run. Tony's suicide attempt (the ultimate control maneuver) had been serious. If she had not become concerned and gone looking for him, he wouldn't be with us now.

In the aftermath of that event, her emotions were still blurred. Tony and Sherry had come to see me to try to salvage their relationship. It was obviously going to be a long and painful process.

It's easy to play armchair quarterback in situations like that, to look back at what happened, but there's one thing I felt confident about: Had Sherry taken certain steps early in their relationship, all the ugliness could have been avoided.

Of all the difficult things I have to say in this book, the most difficult words are directed not to those who control, but to those who let them get away with it. This chapter is for those who find themselves in situations where they are forced to endure the relentless maneuvers of high-control persons. The theme of this chapter is simple, but you're not going to like it, and you may even try to defend yourself by disagreeing with it. But when all is said and done, reality is still reality. High control happens—because we choose to let it happen!

Therefore, one of the most significant persons in bringing freedom where there is presently control is the person under siege.

The Vicious Cycle

People are controlled for the same reasons that people control.

They are afraid. For a complex series of reasons, their innate fear keeps them from standing up to the person controlling them. It can be fear rooted in the past, or perhaps the person controlling them is bigger, more fierce, more powerful, or has authority over them, like a parent. For whatever reasons, fear holds them back from taking deliberate steps to deal with the oppression.

They are angry. They don't know how to deal with their anger, so they do nothing, thinking benign responses are better than the requirements of bitter confrontation.

They are ashamed. The regrets are stacked so high in their hearts that they assume there are no alternatives. Their shame draws their view of themselves so low that they feel unworthy and unfit to be standing in judgment of someone else.

They are in bondage. Their lives are a series of unfortunate choices that have obliterated their resolve. Little spirit or spunk is left—just a disappointment that gnaws away at their confidence. They are convinced that nothing they could do or say would make any difference, so they resign themselves to a life of being coerced and manipulated.

Passivity comes naturally to them. What they do better than anything else is roll with the punches. They're gifted at adaptability and know they're outgunned in a verbal duel, so they don't even try.

To summarize what I've been saying, being controlled is one person's coping mechanism the way controlling is another's. Either way, it's still destructive. Eventually, the emotions hit critical mass, the relationship becomes ground zero, and the explosion that follows leaves little love to salvage. That's what Tony and Sherry found out. He started dominating her from the moment the pastor pronounced them man and wife. And because she allowed it and never took action to stop it, he continued— oblivious to the scars he was leaving on her heart—until one day she'd had enough.

Powerful personalities are the emotional bullies who surround us. They intimidate, dominate, and subjugate. That's why bullies *must* be dealt with. I've had to face a few in my day. Their ability to hurt me was always greater than my ability to hurt in return. Their overbearing presence in my life destroyed my ability to function with freedom. What I had to realize, and what ultimately motivated me to stand up to them, was that as difficult as confrontation was, it could never add up to the long-term damage that would occur if I did nothing. If you're being overcontrolled, you *must* stand up to the controller.

Flawed Belief Systems

Proverbs 23:7 says, *"For as he thinks within himself, so he is."* All our actions and reactions to people, places, and things are rooted in the basic presuppositions we embrace deep within our hearts. These presuppositions are our true belief system. They determine the decisions we make that cause us to either control someone or be controlled.

A woman might believe that the biblical teaching on submission to her husband means he has the right to physically abuse her, so she lets him get away with it. That's a wrong response based on flawed thinking. And the flawed thinking comes from having a flawed belief system. These form the downward spiral that leads to addictive behavior. *Allowing yourself to be controlled is as addictive a pattern as overcontrol.* Let me demonstrate how this works.

Our **belief system** determines our **thinking**
(the conclusions we embrace),
which develops into **addictive behavior.**

Everyone has addictive behavior (in the loose sense of the word). Whether it's healthy or destructive is determined by the belief system behind it—which will either be flawed or truth-based. If our belief system is flawed, it causes our addictive behavior to follow a destructive cycle. It looks like this:

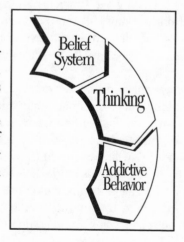

Unhealthy addictive behavior *(allowing ourselves to be controlled)* becomes **a preoccupation** *(we focus on our frustration)*, which causes us to develop **a ritual** *(repeated pattern of coping)* that makes us **compulsive** *(stuck in a behavioral pattern over which we feel we have no control),*which causes **despair.**

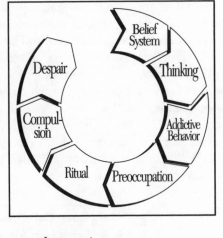

Despair destroys our sense of *personal power*. It throws into motion a series of unhealthy choices to complete the cycle.

Despair *(a sense of helplessness and hopelessness)* leads us to **unmanageable preoccupations** *(overeating, overspending, etc.),* which reinforces **our flawed belief system**[1] *(the self-defeating ways we view ourselves, others, God, and love).*

And so the cycle goes. Our flawed beliefs cause a series of wrong choices that simply reinforce our flawed beliefs. (This works the same way in the controller as it does in the controlled.) What we do is all based on our belief system. Obviously, a person who unfairly dominates another or manipulates him for selfish reasons has something wrong with the way he views himself

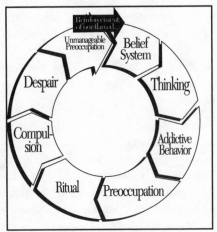

and that other person. He can't possibly be viewing the other individual the way God wants.

All of this leads me to suggest a solution. Whether you're holding the gun or looking down its barrel, relationships in which powerful personalities are allowed to dominate are not what God wants for His children. Therefore, to gain a genuine solution to your nightmare, you need to concentrate on your *belief system*.

To address the many parts of an accurate belief system would take a series of books, and it's not really our purpose here to pick our way through the various nuances of what we believe and how those beliefs cause us to behave. We can be relieved of oppression by narrowing our focus to the one inner dynamic that has the most power to wring out control. For the remainder of our discussion of high control, therefore, we'll look at only one part of our belief system, love, and we'll base our solution on one book: the Bible.

Only Love Can Break a Heart.
Only Love Can Mend It Again.

Love is supposed to be the foundation of our relationships. If our view of love is flawed, our thinking is going to yield unhealthy patterns within our relationships. We'll develop destructive ways of dealing with the people around us.

Paul told husbands, for instance, to *"love your wives, and do not be embittered against them"* (Colossians 3:19). This is difficult to do if our basic presuppositions about love are warped. With all this in mind, then, let's look at some of the faulty views of love that undermine our relationships.

1. Counterfeit Love[2]

Counterfeit love is an external feeling that overwhelms a heart but is not necessarily sustained by adequate knowledge or commitment. When a guy sees a beautiful girl at the beach and says to his friend, "I'm in love," that's counterfeit. What he really means is "I want to own her—to possess her." Many relationships begin with this kind of love, and the people involved allow it to form the foundation of the union that follows. Obviously, if the foundation is faulty, the building cannot stand the test of time.

2. Passive-Agreement Love

Although the Bible tells us to accept people,[3] at no place does it tell us that we have to accept their sin. Passive-agreement love says, "If you really love me, you'll accept my behavior as well as my attitudes. If you don't accept them, you don't love me." When this flawed view of love is implanted in a belief system, it puts the lover in a position of condoning and often being victimized by the other person's sin. Genuine love never requires us to passively accept another person's sin.

3. Lust Love

Lust is any God-given desire carried beyond God's established limits. A guy tells a girl that if she loves him, she'll express her love sexually without requiring a commitment. "Real love," he says, "doesn't need a marriage certificate." This twisted view of love dominates many relationships. It is flawed to the core and leads to painful disappointments. When it is embedded in a belief system, control and countercontrol become a way of life.

4. Consuming Love

Sometimes called "smother love," consuming love is notorious because of its pattern of loving too much. It puts so much expectation on the object or person being loved that the love cannot be sustained. When a husband is his wife's "reason for living," they're going to have problems. Let me show you how this works itself out in families.

• SPOUSE-CENTERED LOVE: Your security is based on the way your spouse responds to you. Such smothering love makes you highly vulnerable and easily disappointed. Anything that competes with the attention you desire from your spouse is perceived as a threat.

• FAMILY-CENTERED LOVE: Your security is based on how well your family accepts you and fulfills your expectations. Your security is only as good as your family's. Your self-esteem, as well as the way you are perceived by others (you think), depends on your family's reputation.

207

• MONEY-CENTERED LOVE: Your security is wrapped up in your net worth. That puts your level of confidence at the mercy of volatile economics.

• WORK-CENTERED LOVE: You use what you *do* to define who you *are*. Therefore, you only feel significant when you're working.

• CHURCH-CENTERED LOVE: Your sense of security is based on your church involvement and the way you're viewed by church leaders.[4]

Smothering love stinks from the inside out. It fails because it's flawed. Obviously, people with consuming love become possessive, which guarantees high control.

5. Enabling Love

We see someone we love engaged in self-destructive behavior. We know it's sinful and harmful for him, and possibly for us. We know he will fall. But our view of love tells us we should be there to cushion him when he crashes. "I'll be there when you fall" sounds great in a love song, but it destroys relationships. If his fall is because of wrong behavior (drug abuse, alcoholism, workaholism, etc.), cushioning the impact of the consequences *encourages* the destructive behavior. When we keep rescuing him, he never feels the impact of his actions enough to admit his need for genuine change.

These flawed forms of love set up base camp in our belief system, move out through our thinking, and show themselves in destructive and addictive behavior. To fix the problem, most people try to adjust their behavior. For a high controller, it might work something like this:

I'm dominating my children. After reading this book, I think I should stop doing this. Therefore, I'm going to start letting them make more choices.

Sounds great! But it's a Band-Aid on an infection. It covers the problem, but it doesn't eliminate it. Regardless of whether it's the controller or the controllee, a change in behavior is only going to work so long. If we want to experience genuine change, we must *change our belief system.* The process for the high controller should work more like this:

I'm dominating my children. There's something deep within me that's fueling this. Perhaps it's fear, maybe I'm angry, or maybe I just let the strength of my personality step over too many lines in their lives. Regardless, I need to try to understand why I've been doing this. Then I need to redefine my view of them so that when I grant them the freedom to make their own choices, it isn't just some cosmetic change within my heart that won't last.

When we build our beliefs on truth, the truths will adjust our thinking. Our changed thinking will enable us to see and change our destructive behavior. This, of course, sounds easy on paper. In reality, it's a process that ·may take a long time. But if we ever want to change, we must turn to a reliable authority and determine what's true and what isn't. God's Word is that kind of authority.

The Source of Our Love

Love, like a river, must have a source. That source can be either polluted or pure. The flawed types of love leave a bitter aftertaste in our relationships. And our thirst for love is never satisfied. There is only one Source we can rely on to give us pure, undefiled love. Listen to John, the disciple "that Jesus loved," describe this source:

> *Beloved, let us love one another, for love is from God; and every one who loves is born of God and knows God. The one who does not love does not know God, for God is love.*
>
> 1 John 4:7-8

Love that does not grow from a heart-to-heart relationship with God cannot sustain us in our day-to-day relationships. Polluted love doesn't last. But those who find their source in God, who is love, are sustained by a love that has no limits.

The Object of Our Love

Without an object, love is meaningless. It's an active force. It must be directed toward someone or something in order to be enjoyed. And the Bible tells us not only who the source of our love should be, but also who the object should be.

Jesus walked into a theological hornets' nest one day when responding to intense questions from some of the most powerful personalities in Israel—the religious power brokers. One particular scribe posed the question: "What commandment is foremost of all?" Jesus gave him the definitive answer by quoting the "Apostles' Creed" of the Old Testament. Listen to the Savior's words:

> *"Hear, O Israel! The Lord our God is one Lord; and you shall love the Lord your God with all your heart, and with all your soul, and with all your mind, and with all your strength." The second is this, "You shall love your neighbor as yourself." There is no other commandment greater than these.*
>
> Mark 12:29-31

Jesus outlined the priority of the objects of our love. The primary object should be the Lord Himself. And He wants us to love Him with everything we've got—our heart, soul, mind, and strength.

Our heart and soul are the center of our emotions and volition.

Our mind enables us to share "reasoned" and "reasonable" love.

Our strength is lived out through action.

Jesus said in these verses that we are to use everything we have to love Him. But if we give everything to God, how can there be anything left to give to anyone else?

Answer: By making God the primary object of our love, we gain from Him the power to love others (the secondary objects of our love) the way we should. The love we receive from Him overwhelms us to such a degree that our capacity to love others cannot be exhausted.

In today's families, moms and dads, sisters and brothers desperately need to put God first. However, in homes held under siege by a powerful personality, it's easy to turn priorities around and love others more than God. A neighbor is anyone whose need I can see and whom I can help. But when we put people (especially those close to us) ahead of Him, we find our capacity to love being quickly depleted.

Let's step back a minute and see how this fits into the big picture.

Someone is controlling me.

I want him to stop.

For that to happen, I need to confront him.

But I feel powerless because of my internal belief system and the intimidation the controller is exercising in my life.

My inability to do anything is based primarily on my flawed view of love.

If I could put love in proper perspective, however, I'd understand that high control poisons relationships.

Therefore, it's imperative that I correct my thinking about love.

The change starts when I make sure my source of love is the Lord. Again, the order is God first, people second.

Now we need to see how our love can be activated in a way that empowers relationships rather than deflating them, and in the process gives us the courage to deal with the controllers in our lives.

The Ingredients of Our Love

When you peel away all the layers of fluff and get down to the core of love, you realize that, at best, it's the toughest and most difficult thing we have to do. Sincere love has a hefty price tag. But unless we pay that price, we will never know the depths of this kind of love.

You love a powerful personality. Maybe it's your husband or wife. Perhaps it's your son, daughter, or an in-law. Even though you love that person, you realize the pressure he's been exerting has strained the relationship and is robbing your joy. Doing nothing will only guarantee the situation will get worse. Like Sherry at the beginning of this chapter, you can deny, trivialize, or do your best to endure the pressure of a powerful personality, but eventually, it gets the best of you. And as long as you do or say nothing, you validate the powerful personality's treatment of you and empower him to keep it up.

Love is the best way to bring relief to your heart. It saves the hostile words, the regrets, the sleepless nights, the loneliness, the tears, and maybe even the attorney's fees. But your love must be on target. When you love God's way, it will be.

I'd like to develop three ingredients our love needs in order to be effective. They are the three strands of a cord necessary to make love strong. Take away even one and the love you desire to give will have a difficult time enduring the pressures it will face. Those three ingredients are tender love, truthful (tough) love, and task love. They are what's needed to free you from the control of a powerful personality. Let's look at them individually and then see how they weave together.

211

The First Ingredient: Tender Love (Using Your Heart)

Elvis's song pleaded for this type of love. For love to be effective, it must first be tender. Tender love prepares the person to receive truthful love. It comes from the heart. *"Fervently love one another from the heart"* (1 Peter 1:22b).

When we cook steaks on the grill, we tenderize them first. This breaks down the tough texture of the meat and allows the seasoning to get in. It not only makes the steak taste better, but it also makes it easier to consume. Putting a steak on the grill without first tenderizing it can ruin it. In the same way, without first being tender, love can ruin your relationship.

You want to voice your concern to your spouse, parent, or child about his high-control behavior. But before you do, you must take a few steps to help "tenderize" the person to receive the truth.

Place high value on the individual.

We need to view the person as God does. His worth to the Father is apparent by how much He was willing to give for him—the life of His own Son on the cross. When we've endured the actions of a high-control individual, it's difficult to have enough affection to remember that in God's eyes the person is extremely valuable. In fact, only by finding our Source of love in the Lord is it possible.

Does the person who's been oppressing you think he's valued by you? What are you doing to communicate you view him as a person of inherent worth? Unless you first affirm that you value him, your motive for doing the other steps will be suspect.

Identify with him.

The second way to show tender love is to empathize with the controller. What hurts might be causing him to flex his muscles at your expense? Are you aware of any fear, anger, shame, or bondage in his life that causes him to protect himself by controlling? Have you prayed for him regarding the disappointments that haunt him? Maybe his controlling attitude is a natural strength that has stepped over the line. Have you thanked God that He chose to give him a strong personality? Have you asked God for help in showing him how to use his natural power in more positive ways?

Unless you get emotionally involved in his life, you can't trust yourself to be fair with him. For instance, living with your teenage son may have become a living nightmare. But what things are happening in his life that might have contributed to his caustic shift in behavior? Has he been jilted by friends? Have you given him help to make wise choices? Maybe he's feeling awkward, lonely, stupid, or scared. The more you can isolate the things that fuel his pain, the more you can understand his control.

Try to communicate at his level.

The third way to love tenderly is to communicate at the person's level. I don't mean "talk his language." However, your kids, your spouse, and your parents all have avenues through which it's easier for them to communicate.

If you take a 300-pound tackle for an NFL team, put him in a delivery room, and let him watch his wife give birth to a tiny son or daughter, you'll see him transform. This powerful man who loves to rearrange people's heads for fun suddenly turns to gelatin. He'll cradle that infant in his massive arms and coo softly toward its sleeping eyes while tears drip down his cheeks. He doesn't know what the child is thinking, but he's certain the child won't respond favorably if he uses his normal, intimidating voice.

What things does your spouse most enjoy? What excites your children? What areas of interest are drawing your parents' focus? Knowing these areas will help you communicate. Even though you don't know a lot about those interests and may not be able to speak to them as well as you'd like, you are nonetheless showing your concern. That tenderizes a person's heart.

The Second Ingredient: Truthful Love (Using Your Head)

Truthful love is based on the scriptural principle that says, *"[Love] does not rejoice in unrighteousness, but rejoices with the truth"* (1 Corinthians 13:6).

Truthful love is often referred to as "tough love" because it's so difficult to practice. As the cliché says, the truth hurts. But without it your love's a sham, and eventually it won't hold up. You may endure the relationship, but it won't be love. Many couples were in love for the first few years of their marriage but spent the next 50 just tolerating each other. As the Nike ad says, "Life is short. Play hard." How do you play hard when it comes to truthfully loving the powerful personalities in your life? By *confronting* them with their inappropriate behavior.

You may not know the perfect method to use in a particular crisis, but you must not let that stop you from doing *something*.

When I was in graduate school, I took tennis lessons from an experienced pro, Walter Senior. I was obsessed with the "killer shot." I wanted to place the ball at the perfect spot on the opponent's court every time. But Walter said to me several times, "Tim, don't preoccupy yourself with getting the perfect shot; just make sure you put it in the other guy's court. Whether it's the perfect shot or not, once it's on his side, he has to deal with it."

While you're working to put the ball in the high controller's court, here are some things to keep in mind.

• *Make sure you confront with facts, not feelings.* If you say to your spouse, "I feel that you tyrannize me and you're destroying our marriage," you won't get far. That's too general. Be specific. "Your rage frightens me. When you yell at me and approach me aggressively, you make me think you're going to physically harm me. I need to know: Is that what you want to do—hurt me?"

Now the ball's in his court. Two facts are inescapable: His volume and actions are aggressive, and they frighten you. You've now called him into responsibility for what he's doing.

I chose that example because it is one in which the person might turn volatile over the confrontation. If he does, it's obvious you're in an abusive environment, and regardless of the inconvenience to you, you should get yourself (and your children) out of it until he agrees to seek help. Don't be afraid to tell him his actions leave you no choice. Let him bear the consequences for those actions. That's putting the responsibility in the lap of the person who should be assuming it anyway. In violent situations, it's best to exercise truthful love in a place where you're safe (or with someone nearby who will protect you).

Many other types of power, however, aren't violent. When you confront on these, be just as specific.

Husband to wife: "Ever since I told you we don't have enough money for you to go visit your sister, you've withdrawn from me sexually. That was over two months ago. This is not only frustrating to me, but it has also caused me a lot of concern about where we are as a couple. It could point to some serious problems we need to deal with. Is there any connection between the foiled trip to your sister's house and the fact that we haven't made love for two months? If not, why have you turned away from me lately?"

There may be no connection between the two. But specific actions have placed the dilemma before the wife in such a way that she has to look at what she's doing.

• *Be direct, but don't judge.* If you tell a controller you think he's a jerk, you may feel better, but you're no closer to a resolution of the problem. Withholding judgment minimizes retaliation, and being direct places his actions where the person must respond to them. Let's consider a teenage daughter approaching her domineering mother.

"Mother, you've chosen my courses at school for the last three years. You've placed me in accelerated courses that have been extremely demanding. I haven't been given an opportunity to participate in the direction of my academic interests. This has made me feel a lot of grief, plus resentment toward you. Because you're my mother, I'll submit to your leadership in this area of my life, but it's hurting my ability to trust you. Is there any compromise we can make?"

The mom now knows how her actions are affecting her daughter. She also realizes she's fueling frustration between herself and her daughter. Even if she chooses not to change, her daughter has relieved herself from being a benign enabler of her mother's dominance. By articulating the issues, the daughter has placed the responsibility for the relationship at the mom's feet. For the daughter, this can be the first of many honest statements that will enable her to gain emotional emancipation from her mother. When the daughter finally leaves home and is on her own, her mother will be less likely to or capable of controlling her.

One of the ways to tell if you're being judgmental is to ask yourself if you gain any joy from telling the controller the truth. If the truth is painful to him, it should also be painful to you because of your love for him.

• *Risk your status in the person's eyes for the sake of his well-being.* Assume, going in, that the high controller won't fall at your feet in contrition and repentance. That's why you have to be motivated by more than your own best interests. You genuinely have to have his benefit in your heart, too. That will help you hold to your guns when he reacts. He may scream, get angry, cry, or try to make you feel guilty. Those all go with the territory of confrontation. But by taking action against his behavior and holding him responsible for it, you place him in the best position to have the Lord work on his heart.

Confrontation means letting someone hurt enough to want to get well. It means letting the crisis happen to him without erasing any of the painful consequences. It also means that when he's hurting from the consequences of his actions, you don't intervene to soften them.

Mothers are notorious for circumventing the harsh consequences of their children's poor judgment. Softening the consequences only postpones the cure. We must be willing to stand firm even if they reject us in the process.

That's a hard pill to swallow, so let me mention something that might make it go down a little easier: People who play you like a pawn on a chessboard are really demonstrating a subtle form of rejection. By circumventing the consequences of their actions, you're letting them reject you even more.

I need to point out that sometimes the confrontation may not change the behavior, but it can alleviate anxiety nonetheless. When you're being pushed around, you feel as angry about your inability (or unwillingness) to do anything about it as you do about the offense. Confrontation empowers you, simply because you've finally refused to continue being a victim. A high-control spouse may continue the control, or an in-law may continue trying to run your marriage, but now you will respond differently because you've stopped allowing others to control you without being held accountable.

All of this can be very painful. Most corrective surgery is. When your relationship heals, however, it will be better than you ever imagined.

The Third Ingredient: Task Love (Using Your Hands)

First John 3:18 says, *"Let us not love with [merely] word or with tongue, but in deed and truth."* Task love moves us from being confronters to being participants in the cure. This is where our love becomes self-sacrificing. Most of us are good either at being tender or telling people the truth. We need to be both—in balance. Then we must follow these with activity directed toward loving the person at his greatest point of need.

Paul Harvey told the story of Larry Trapp on his radio program. Larry was a grand dragon in the Ku Klux Klan in Lincoln, Nebraska. He seethed with hatred toward blacks and Jews. And the biggest target of his wrath was a Jewish rabbi named Weisman.

Although Weisman had never met Larry Trapp, he had no doubt that he was hated by him. Trapp used all the sick methods for which hate mongers are notorious. His campaign sent fear to every part of Weisman's being. But what Trapp didn't realize when he decided to hate Weisman was that this dear rabbi had great love for his fellow man—even Larry Trapp. This love motivated Weisman to do some research into his enemy.

Weisman discovered that Trapp was a double amputee. Then he decided to apply a "Christian" principle and do good to the man who was mistreating him. He started calling Trapp's house. Trapp refused to talk. Because of the rabbi's persistence, however, one day Trapp finally conversed with him.

Rabbi Weisman asked if Trapp needed any help going to the grocery store or doing chores. Trapp hung up. The rabbi called again. This time Trapp used every profane expression he could think of to describe his hatred for this Jew. Then he hung up.

Because love constrained him, Weisman continued to offer his help. Weeks passed. The phone kept ringing, and the conversations became less hostile. Eventually Trapp consented to let Weisman do some shopping for him.

Ultimately, love won out. Larry Trapp quit the Ku Klux Klan, got rid of all his hate tracts and pamphlets, and became a close friend with the man he had once devoted his waking hours to despising. When asked what happened, Trapp said, "When you get love like that, you can only give it back."

How can you take an active part in loving the person who's controlling you? Getting involved in hands-on love lends credibility to the love you give from your heart and your head.

Grace-Based Reconciliation

God wants you to enjoy relationships uncompromised and unblemished by the manipulative power of overcontrol. That happens when you let Him use your heart, then your head, and ultimately your hands. It doesn't come easily or quickly, but with God's help it can come. Loving with God as your Source will give you a clearer purpose. Even if you can't change the situations you're enduring, you can tap the unlimited patience of God's love to see you through.

In the end, you will sense God's grace in your life. The voids caused by disappointments you've had to face can give way to fulfilling love. And the steps you take to love people "God's way" will not be in vain. That love is infinite and active. It has been doing miracles for thousands of years. It can do one for you.

Don't wait until all you have are regrets. Free up your kids, your spouse, and yourself. Let God's grace rule in your family, and put the tyranny of powerful personalities behind you for good.

101 Ways to Identify and Manage a High Controller

How to Identify a High Controller, Even If It's You

1. There's nothing like owing money to put yourself in a position of being controlled. Avoid borrowing money from parents, relatives, or friends.

2. He's a controller if he always has to have the last word.

3. She's a controller if she chooses silence and withdrawal instead of communication.

4. You're being controlled if no matter how hard you try, you can never get it right.

5. You're being controlled if a single glance from your partner can change your mind.

6. If you think, *It's all up to me*, you're probably a high controller.

7. If you think, *They never seem to get it right*, you're probably a high controller.

8. If people tend to defer to you as the last word on their plans and dreams, undoubtedly you are a high controller.

9. If when you pray, you suggest solutions to God, you could be a high controller.

10. If he says, "Of course I'll respect you in the morning," two things are certain: First, he's trying to control you, and second, he won't respect you in the morning. Tell him to "take a hike."

11. Good guilt is designed to turn you from your sinful ways. Bad guilt is designed to manipulate you. If someone is trying to heap bad guilt on you, refuse to submit to his attempt to control you.

12. Alcoholics and drug users are high controllers. If you go along with an abuser of drugs and alcohol, and do nothing to break the pattern of abuse, you're asking to be controlled.

13. Sex can be used to control another. Never use sex as a method of getting your own way.

14. An understanding of the Scriptures, without an understanding of God's grace could cause you to use the Bible to control other people.

15. The prefix *Reverend* before a name is not a license to control other people.

16. Using the Bible to get your own way is a form of control, and you are probably breaking the third commandment, which forbids taking the Lord's name in vain.

17. You're high controlling when you follow favors with requests—"Here's $100. By the way ..."

18. High controllers often have hidden agendas, which almost always hurt others. For the sake of those you love, tell them what's on your mind.

19. Prenuptial agreements are a form of high control because they say, if you don't perform as you promised, I'll divorce you.

20. When people control you they are showing they don't respect you.

21. Don't let the majority control what you believe. The majority doesn't determine truth. Even if a million people believe a lie, it's still a lie. Let truth be your guide.

22. Clothes and hood ornaments don't make the man. Character does. If the only way you feel you can relate to people is by letting them tell you what success is, you're being controlled and your success is an illusion.

23. Avoid setting personal goals that require the cooperation of the people you love, because if they don't comply with your plan, you might be inclined to control them into compliance.

24. If there's more than one way to skin a cat, then there's got to be more than one way to do just about anything else. "Do it my way or hit the highway" is a nasty form of high control.

25. There's little about raising children that's convenient. If high control is the method you've chosen to lighten your burden as a parent, you've obviously misunderstood your position.

26. Setting people up for failure is a way to control them. If they don't know what to do, and you don't teach them, they will fail.

27. It is absolutely essential that the people you love have the freedom to make mistakes. Otherwise, you're controlling them.

28. The surest way to have your children stay financially dependent on you long after they've left home is to control them by making most of their decisions when they are small.

29. If your parents or in-laws are trying to control your marriage, move to the opposite side of the country for about 50 years.

30. Violence is an ultimate attempt to control. If anyone ever threatens violence against you, get help immediately.

31. Observe your children's friendships. If you notice them controlling their friends, train them out of that pattern. You'll probably save them from divorce.

32. Observe your children's friendships. If you notice them *being* controlled, train them out of that pattern. Once again, you'll probably save them from divorce.

33. Strong-willed children, if brought up right, can have an incredible impact for God's cause. The key to strong-willed children is that they want to have some control of what's going on in their lives. Without surrendering one bit of authority as a parent, you can still let them pick what they want from a restaurant menu, the outfit they want to wear, which bed they want to take a nap in, and so forth. Choose your battles carefully or it will become one high controller pitted against another. In most cases, you'll lose.

34. Generous usage of personal possessive pronouns is a sign of high controllers. "My money, my secretary, my idea, my way," are all expressions used by them. If you're dating someone who uses "my" all the time, beware.

35. If someone is *demanding* your honor and respect, he is a high controller. Honor and respect can't be demanded. They have to be earned.

36. Two things in life don't last: toys bought at a dollar store and high-control relationships that go unchecked.

37. A paycheck is the result of services rendered. It does not give your employer the right to control your personal life.

38. If you can't articulate your spouse's three greatest dreams, you've probably been exercising undue control.

39. There might be 50 ways to leave your lover, but there is just one simple way to cause your lover to want to leave you—control him.

40. High controllers often wear masks to hide their vulnerabilities. It's called image control. Ultimately, time exposes us for what we are. Be authentic, warts and everything, because when all is said and done, you end up with authentic relationships which can stand a lifetime of challenges.

41. Most people abuse by negatively controlling people around them.

42. A high controller often takes charge even when it is not his responsibility to do so. It is often because he doesn't trust other people's ability to make things turn out right.

43. When you are afraid to voice your opinion to someone, suspect high-control is happening.

44. True love, free from control, places a high value on the individual. If you do not feel valued as a person, you are probably experiencing control.

How to Manage a High Controller, Even If It's You

45. Release control of your children a little at a time by giving them ownership of as many assets as you can as soon as you can.

46. Get out of debt, because those to whom you owe money may decide to control you until your debt is paid.

47. Instead of trying to win an argument just so you can be in control, seek understanding.

48. When it comes to your kids, strive to keep them under control rather than controlling them.

49. When in-laws and parents seek to control your family by insisting you spend holidays with them, it's time to start your own family traditions.

50. Never allow anyone to strike you in anger. Such action is a form of controlling violence. If it happens, get help.

51. When fear drives you to control, claim the promise in John 14:27: "Peace I leave with you; my peace I give you. I do not give to you as the world gives. Do not let your hearts be troubled and do not be afraid."

52. Rule of thumb: If you go through each day assuming you're capable of being a high controller, you are more apt to be watching for it and correcting it when it rears its ugly head.

53. Most anger results from blocked expectations. The fewer expectations you have of others, the less anger you will have toward them, and the less chance there is for you to try to control them.

54. If someone's anger causes him to try to control you, find out what expectation has been blocked, and if it is legitimate, try to meet it.

55. We tend to control more when we're tired. For everyone's sake, guard your rest.

56. Courage is a prerequisite for facing down high controllers. Pray for large doses of it.

57. When building new relationships, don't give people permission to control you. The first time they try it, stand up to them. In the majority of cases, they'll back down. If those relationships were meant to be, they will grow from that point, on a much better platform. If those individuals reject you because you won't let them control, then count your blessings and move on with life.

58. If you absolutely need someone's approval so much that you're willing to let him exercise unfair control in your life, then you need to go to the foot of the cross and remind yourself what happened there. Find the source of your life in Christ, then you won't have to jeopardize your heart in order to find fulfillment in life.

59. Standing up to a high controller takes courage. We lack courage when our fears get the best of us. The best way to cast out a bad fear is to have a good fear. Start with the fear of God. When you fear God more, you'll fear men less.

60. Temper tantrums are a form of high control. If you give in to someone having a temper tantrum, he will only continue and

his tantrums will get more sophisticated as time goes on. Your two best options are either to ignore a temper tantrum, or to respond with discipline.

61. High-control supervisors could make life miserable for you if you let them control you or if you *refuse* to let them control you. For the sake of your career, keep verifiable notes on any infractions against you.

62. A great definition of love is: the commitment of my will to your needs and best interests, regardless of the cost to me. If you genuinely love someone, it's not in his best interest to allow him to control you.

63. When kids moan and whine, they're attempting to control you. You'll do them and their future a big favor by refusing to tolerate this behavior.

64. Develop weekly "staff meetings" with your spouse. Together, go over the details of your family life. Good communication and common goals decrease the need for control.

65. Give your children an outlet for their anger so that they don't feel controlled. A good option is "What's Your Beef" night. (See page 171 for more help on this subject.)

66. Resist the urge to rescue your children from the consequences of their poor choices. In the long run, you'll save them from using manipulation and control to get their way and you'll build them into better people.

67. If you're asked to lie for someone, don't do it, no matter who it is. He's trying to control you.

68. If you don't control your credit card, it will control you.

69. If you are tall and you have to exchange difficult words with others, you might be using your height as a control device. Always come down to their eye level. Either bend down, sit down, or if they're children, get down on your knees.

70. Since anger increases our physical strength, we must never try to control a child by spanking him when we are angry.

71. They say "silence is golden." Sometimes it's yellow. If your convictions are telling you to speak up, then *speak up!* Stop being controlled by fear.

72. Some men like their wives to take care of them the way their mothers did, but they don't want to be treated as children. This is one more form of control. Make a deal with your husband that you'll respond to him as a wife, period.

73. One of the most loving answers you can give a high controller is, "no."

74. Refuse to allow your family's taste buds to be controlled by the market place or Madison Avenue.

75. Make a list of everyone who has hurt you. Go through that list in prayer every day and ask God for the power to forgive. Keep doing this until their infractions against your heart cease compelling you to control.

76. Give the people you love the freedom to be a little weird.

77. "Please" is another way of saying "I respect you," and it defuses a potentially controlling situation.

78. Avoid the temptation to high control a friend by refusing to loan money to him. Either *give* him the money or introduce him to your banker.

79. Life is too short to spend it working in a high-control environment for someone you can't stand. Think abundantly and go find a new job.

80. There's a two-to-one ratio between your ears and your mouth. Listen twice as much as you talk and you may avoid saying something that is controlling.

81. Family secrets make high controllers out of everyone in the family. Bring the truth into the light. Admit what needs to be admitted and then move on with your life. The negative

impact of a shotgun wedding, an abortion, a bankruptcy, a felony, or an annulment isn't even remotely close to the devastation caused by the high-control tendencies needed to keep these things secrets.

82. Remember: When you give up the need to control someone and forgive him, you're simply letting him off *your* hook. He's still on *God's* hook.

83. Stay close to God. It's difficult to maintain freed-up relationships without a daily relationship with God, who sets us totally free.

84. Close friendships don't come cheap. A friendship can only be close if the parties involved don't feel smothered—controlled.

85. Jesus never exercised control over anyone. Go thou and do likewise.

86. The practice of consistently saving money may be your only salvation from a high-control job situation.

87. Always strive to improve yourself. The better you are, the less need you'll have to control others. And the better you are, the less others will feel free to control you.

88. Remember: You can choose your actions or you can choose your consequences, but you can't choose both. One determines the other.

89. The worst thing you could do to someone you love deeply is to hate his control over you and yet say nothing about it.

90. Your choice to free people to be the best they can possibly be will cause you to exhibit grace-based actions toward them. Living in grace is the opposite of controlling others.

91. If you are in a situation where there is absolutely no way you can free yourself from the tyranny of a high controller because the consequences would be too dangerous, pray for God's mercy and grace. He gave it to Joseph when he was in prison. He gave it to Shadrach, Meshach, and Abednego when they were in the fiery furnace. He gave it to Daniel in the lions' den.

He gave it to Paul in prison and to John while he was in exile. He'll give it to you, too.

92. If you are a high controller, consider taking to heart the scripture that says, "Whoever wants to become great among you must be your servant" (Matt. 20:26).

93. Healthy, control-free relationships are held together by grace, not by guilt.

94. Shame is the master emotion, the unseen regulator of our entire affective life. If you or someone you know is experiencing shame, look farther, because something is wrong. At the core of a controller's heart is his sense of utter shame that blocks his ability to see himself as anything but fundamentally and absolutely flawed.

95. A lack of honesty indicates a lack of trust, and a lack of trust means someone is controlling others. It's time to seek help from a professional who can reveal the truth of the situation.

96. People who exercise a high degree of unnecessary control are either afraid, angry, ashamed, or in bondage to something. To the degree that you can help them overcome their fear, get rid of their anger, release themselves from their shame, or free themselves from the things that enslave them, you help them and you help yourself.

97. Give someone close to you, someone you trust, permission to tell you every time you exercise undue control over another person.

98. In the matter of in-laws. Removing yourself from the proximity of high-control in-laws doesn't mean you don't love or respect them. It does mean, however, that you are willing to carry out your stewardship before God and not allow their high control to infect your marriage.

99. Confront a high controller with specific facts, not feelings. If he reacts with anger and hostility, you are in an abusive situation and need to get away to protect your life.

100. When we hold all God has given us in an open palm, He is not only free to use us, but also to empower the precious people He allows us to serve.

101. The way to stop controlling or being controlled is to change our belief systems. The way we do that is by discovering truth. High-control poisons relationships, but love rebuilds them, and God is love.

Endnotes

Chapter Two

1. Lance Morrow, "The Bright Cave Under the Hat," *Time* (December 24, 1990), p. 78.

Chapter Three

1. Barbara Sullivan, *The Control Trap* (Minneapolis: Bethany House Publishers, 1991), p. 44.
2. Ibid.
3. Ibid. (adapted from pp. 44-45).

Chapter Four

1. Barbara DeAngelis, *Secrets About Men Every Woman Should Know* (New York: Delacorte Press, 1990), p. 31.
2. Barbara Sullivan, *The Control Trap* (Minneapolis: Bethany House Publishers, 1991), p. 50.
3. See Ephesians 6:1.
4. See Ephesians 5:23.

5. *Webster's New Collegiate Dictionary* (Springfield, Massachusetts: G & C Merriam Company, 1979) p. 742.
6. Robert M. Bramson, *Coping With Difficult People* (New York: Doubleday, 1981), p. 12.
7. Ibid., p. 37.
8. See Acts 16:31.

Chapter Five
1. Robert M. Bramson, *Coping With Difficult People* (New York: Doubleday, 1981), p. 145.
2. Ibid., p. 89-90.

Chapter Six
1. Robert M. Bramson, *Coping With Difficult People* (New York: Doubleday, 1981), p. 52.

Chapter Seven
1. If you want to read how to build courage into your family, you might want to peek at my book, *Homegrown Heroes: How to Raise Courageous Kids*, by Tim Kimmel, (Portland: Multnomah Press, 1992.)

Chapter Eight
1. See Ephesians 4:26.
2. Milton Layton, *Escaping the Hostility Trap* (Englewood Cliffs, New Jersey: Prentice Hall, Inc., 1977), p. 196.
3. Frederick Buechner, *Wishful Thinking: A Theological ABC* (New York: Harper & Row, 1973), p. 2.
4. Paul J. Gelinas, *Coping with Anger* (New York: The Rosen Publishing Group, Inc. 1979), p.15.
5. For an excellent discussion on how to resolve anger, see Gary Rosberg, *Choosing to Love Again* (Colorado Springs, Colorado: Focus on the Family Publishing, 1992).

Chapter Nine
1. Robert Karen "Shame," *The Atlantic Monthly* (February, 1992), p.40.
2. Barbara Sullivan, *The Control Trap* (Minneapolis: Bethany House Publishers, 1991), p. 103.

3. Robert Karen, "Shame," *The Atlantic Monthly* (February 1992), p. 47.
4. Ibid., p. 43.
5. Merle A. Fossum & Marilyn J. Mason, *Facing Shame* (New York: W. W. Norton & Company, 1986), p. 44.
6. Ibid., p. xii.
7. See Genesis 3: 7-10.

Chapter Ten
1. If you want to get in contact with Neil Anderson's ministry, or wish to get a catalog of his excellent books on the subject, write to: Freedom in Christ Ministries, 491 E. Lambert Road, La Habra, CA 90631.
2. See Ephesians 6: 10-18.

Chapter Eleven
1. The best treatment of this information is found in a book by Gary Smalley and Dr. John Trent, *The Two Sides of Love* (Colorado Springs: Focus on the Family Publishers, 1990.) It will help you know how to bring out the best in each other.

Chapter Twelve
1. Chuck and Barb Snyder, *Incompatibility: Grounds for a Great Marriage* (Sisters, OR: Questar, 1988.)
2. Tim Kimmel, *Homegrown Heroes: How to Raise Courageous Kids* (Multnomah Press: Portland, 1992) p. 67-68.

Chapter Thirteen
1. W. Peter Blitchington, *Sex, Roles & The Christian Family*, (Wheaton, IL., Tyndale House Publishers, Inc. 1984), p. 51.
2. Tim Kimmell, *Little House on the Freeway* (Portland: Multnomah Press, 1987), p. 155.
3. Barbara DeAngelis, *Secrets About Men Every Women Should Know* (New York: Bantam Doubleday Dell Publishing Group, Inc., 1990), p. 128.
4. Ibid., p. 165.
5. "You've Got a Friend" by Carole King.

Chapter Fourteen

1. Tim Kimmel, *Raising Kids Who Turn Out Right* (Sisters, OR: Questar, 1993.)
2. Barbara Sullivan, *The Control Trap* (Minneapolis: Bethany House Publishers, 1991), p. 189.
3. See Mark 6:30-32.
4. Digby Wolfe, adapted from his poem, "Here's to Kids Who are Different."

Chapter Sixteen

1. See John 8:32.
2. See Joshua 7.

Chapter Seventeen

1. Much appreciation is extended to Glenn Rosenberger who gave me an afternoon out of his busy schedule to show me this valuable insight into human behavior.
2. I'm indebted to the marvelous work of Dr. David W. Miller, of The Church at Rocky Peak, his audio message "Love: Giving My Heart, Head, and Hands!" (Chatsworth, CA: 1992) for many of these concepts on love.
3. See Romans 14:1; 15:7.
4. Adapted from Stephen R. Covey, *The Seven Habits of Highly Effective People* (New York: Simon and Schuster: 1989), pp. 119-121.